D0887107

"You Should Be Grateful"

"You Should Be Grateful"

STORIES OF RACE, IDENTITY, AND TRANSRACIAL ADOPTION

ANGELA TUCKER

BEACON PRESS, BOSTON

BEACON PRESS
Boston, Massachusetts
www.beacon.org

Beacon Press books
are published under the auspices of
the Unitarian Universalist Association of Congregations.

26 25 24 23   8 7 6 5 4 3 2 1

This book is printed on acid-free paper that meets the uncoated paper
ANSI/NISO specifications for permanence as revised in 1992.

Text design and composition by Kim Arney

Library of Congress Cataloging-in-Publication Data is available for this title.
ISBN: 978-0-8070-0651-1
E-book: 978-0-8070-0652-8; audiobook: 978-0-8070-0836-2

This book is for all adoptees who have ever felt hiraeth.

HIRAETH (here-eyeth), noun. A deep yearning for a home that never was.

On Children

Your children are not your children.
They are the sons and daughters of Life's longing for itself.
They come through you but not from you,
And though they are with you yet they belong not to you.

You may give them your love but not your thoughts,
For they have their own thoughts.
You may house their bodies but not their souls,
For their souls dwell in the house of tomorrow,
which you cannot visit, not even in your dreams.
You may strive to be like them, but seek not to make them like you.
For life goes not backward nor tarries with yesterday.
You are the bows from which your children as living arrows are sent forth.
The archer sees the mark upon the path of the infinite,
and He bends you with His might that His arrows may go swift and far.
Let your bending in the archer's hand be for gladness;
For even as He loves the arrow that flies, so He loves also the bow that is stable.

—KAHLIL GIBRAN, The Prophet

CONTENTS

ADOPTEE MANIFESTO

AN ADOPTEE MANIFESTO

We can love more than one set of parents.
Relationships with our birth parents, foster parents, and our
adoptive parents are not mutually exclusive.
We have the right to own our original birth certificate.
Curiosity about our roots is innate.
We need access to our family medical history.
The pre-verbal memories you have with your first family are real.
Post-natal Culture Shock exists.
It's okay to feel a mixture of gratitude and loss.
We are not alone.
We have each other.

THERE ARE SEVEN MILLION ADOPTEES IN THE WORLD. Six out of every ten Americans have a "personal experience" with adoption.[1] Yet the concept of adoptee centrism may be unfamiliar. I'd like to introduce you to the concept because it's the lens through which I've written this book. Centering adoptee voices is very important to me because adoptive parents are overwhelmingly represented in adoption dialogue, laws, and public perception, and oftentimes adoptive parents unwittingly direct their own children's narratives. I don't believe that a full understanding and education about adoption can be had without listening to adoptees' firsthand perspectives of what it means to be adopted. In November 2014, I participated in the #FlipTheScript social media movement—a movement started by Rosita González, a Korean adoptee, with the simple goal of amplifying adoptee voices during National Adoption Awareness Month. The campaign reached thirty million households in thirty days! This was both thrilling and saddening, because as we began to speak out, we were often shut down by those who demanded that we should just be grateful for being adopted. The word *should* has always irked me. In a therapy session I unearthed the reason why the word is frustrating. It feels like a combination of judgment and failure—like I was doing something wrong before I'd even expressed anything. And it was often said by people who meant well and had the kindest of intentions. It wasn't meant to be a judgment statement. But it was.

I have had the great fortune to talk about adoptees' rights, including in my 2013 documentary *Closure*, which recounts the search for my birth parents and which streamed on Netflix, Hulu, iTunes, Amazon Prime, and KweliTV. I've produced *The Adoptee Next Door* podcast, three short films about open adoptions, and a three-part web series featuring interviews with transracially adopted youth. I've enjoyed consulting with the writers of NBC's show *This Is Us* and the Tony Award–winning Broadway show *Jagged Little Pill* to ensure that the fictional adoptee characters were accurately represented. These opportunities, along with my blog, *The Adopted Life*, have led to my great privilege of speaking to more than ten thousand adoptees in forty-five states, seven countries, and five continents about their experiences, concerns, fears, and dreams as they chart a course through the complicated experience of adoption.

I've drawn from these experiences to populate some of the stories in this book. The adoptees whose stories you'll read within these pages were all adopted by American families. Some joined their new families through domestic adoption like me, some through international adoption. Beyond geography, we are connected by questions of who we are and where we come from—questions that are harder than you might think to answer because, for many of us, our origins are a mystery. Some of the names have been changed in this book. Dialogue is rendered as best as I can remember it or from journal entries that I wrote after the encounter.

In this book, you may notice me ducking and dodging with my words. That's because being honest about adoption is a tricky minefield to navigate. Writing honestly about adoption seems to inevitably hurt someone or to risk being misconstrued. A common through line is for adoptees to conceal their burdens from their adoptive family to make everyone around them comfortable. For this reason, it was quite difficult to write this book. A connection to my birth family was always important to me, as was having access to my medical history. But the more I was dissuaded by folks who told me to "just be grateful for the family I have!" the more it fueled me. It fueled me to write the manifesto as a way to affirm my reality in a society that was pushing back against it at every turn. I've spent countless hours convincing others and myself that each of the statements in my manifesto matter and have legitimacy. After I wrote *An Adoptee Manifesto*, I had it designed and framed and hung it on my wall to help remind me of my rights.

It must be noted that this is not a how-to book; nor is there a pro-adoption or anti-adoption slant. This book does not prescribe a future of the very complex world of transracial adoption; nor do I speak on behalf of all adoptees. Instead, I'm seeking to raise your consciousness about the adoption industry by sharing the stories of some adoptees. It is my hope that this book will ensure that our society values the lived and varied experiences of adoptees.

PART I

DISCOVERING

CHAPTER 1

YOU SHOULD BE GRATEFUL

"**G**OOD MORNING! THANK YOU for coming today." From my spot behind the black curtain I can't see the person who is introducing me, but her voice resounds through the auditorium. No matter how many times I give keynote speeches, I still get butterflies in my stomach just before I'm introduced. My phone buzzes in my pocket and I panic for a second realizing I forgot to put it on Do Not Disturb before my talk. I fumble it from my pocket and am instantly soothed to see a text message from Bryan, who is filming a documentary two states away. Of all the things I love about my husband, his ability to know exactly when I need an encouraging text may be my favorite. "You got this, my love! Call me after you're done."

"Maybe you saw her on Anderson Cooper, watched the documentary *Closure* on Netflix and bawled all the way through it like I did, or perhaps saw her tussle with Jada Pinkett Smith when explaining the complexities of being a Black woman raised by white people. Please join me in welcoming our keynote speaker, the velvet hammer, transracial adoptee, Angela . . ." I don't wait to hear my last name before striding onto the stage, timing the entrance for ultimate effect. My foot slips for a second. *Perhaps I shouldn't have worn these three-inch heels?* I shorten my steps a bit to ensure I don't end up on my face in front of the hundreds of people gathered in the auditorium. But glancing down at those patent leather beauties I decide I'm pleased with my impulse purchase, and the combination of my Lemonade braids (a cornrowed hairstyle), fuschia-pink lipstick, and gold hoop earrings have me feeling powerful and ready to deliver my speech.

"Thank you so much for inviting me here today." I lean into the mic and stare out into a sea of faces, mostly obscured by the bright spotlight, before launching in to deliver my remarks. "I had everything I needed to fulfill the American Dream—a loving middle-class family, great education, and a plethora of opportunities. But as a Black, transracial adoptee growing up in a white community, I struggled to feel a true sense of belonging. My adoption was closed, which meant I had no legal rights to know my birth family or the circumstances surrounding my birth and adoption. I'm sure you've heard the Oreo analogy? If not, this is where peers accuse people like me of being 'Black on the outside and white on the inside.'"

As usual, once I'm behind the podium, my nerves fall away. I no longer need to refer to my notes. I'm gliding along a smooth groove, sharing with confidence and pride. I dive into the details of my story with gusto. Although more than 50 percent of people who experience infertility consider adoption, this was not the motivation for my parents.[1] Instead, they felt compelled by the teachings of the Zero Population Growth (ZPG; known today as Population Connection) group, a popular pro-environment organization from the 1970s, which posited: "The mother of the year should be a sterilized woman with two adopted children."[2] The core message sought to establish a link between population growth and environmental degradation. The primary tenets of the ZPG were not that humans should stop procreating but that women should be educated and empowered to be in control of their fertility. This message resonated so strongly with my soon-to-be adoptive parents that they built their entire family around it, adopting seven children, giving birth to one biologically—or *homemade*, as my dad likes to say—and welcoming countless foster children into our home as well. They held on to five core principles that they desired for all their children—whether adopted, homemade, or fostered. They wanted all their children to be voters, readers, high school graduates, travelers, and kind.

I press the clicker to control my slideshow to display a family picture on the huge screen behind me. It's a veritable 1990s time capsule: my mom wearing a red sweater with shoulder pads, her brown hair shaped like Sally Field of *Forrest Gump*, one of my sisters has a Rachel (from *Friends*) hairstyle, one of my brothers has his Afro shaped like Kid's from Kid 'n Play, the hip-hop group that was popular in the early '90s, and my dad standing confidently giving off Richard Dreyfuss from *Mr. Holland's*

Opus vibes. I stood with my enormous and perpetual smile, while wearing a sweatshirt embroidered with the name of my birth city, Chattanooga, Tennessee. A small murmur of chuckles rises from the audience. I am sure the laughter is innocent and not meant to harm, but I can't resist the teachable moment. "You are not the first people to laugh at us," I note wryly, and the laughter immediately ceases. "I'm sure you were chuckling at our excellent fashion choices," I reassure them. "But growing up in the small city of Bellingham, Washington, in the '90s meant that our transracially adopted family received a lot of stares and disrespectful utterances. This was not a place accustomed to seeing mixed-race families in their midst." The mood of the room returned to one of rapt attention.

The fascination bestowed on families like mine typically came from the carryover of adoptions from the mid-1990s and the emphasis adoption agencies placed on matching. Blond-haired, blue-eyed children were sent to live with blond-haired, blue-eyed adults. The belief was that life would be easier for a child if they were placed with a family that looked like them, and it'd be easier on the whole family as well. There would be no intrusive questions or sideways stares, because nothing looked out of the ordinary. Visible differences inferred incompatibility. Adopted children were approached as blank slates, a theory popularized in 1929 by Georgia Tann, the executive director of the Tennessee Children's Home Society. The Blank Slate theory was developed as a method to make children more "marketable." It was Tann's assertion that the babies she provided to adoptive couples could be molded into the couples' own image and preferences.[3] It was assumed that the adoptees would assimilate into their new family without any pushback.

It wasn't just about looks though. There was also a drive to match families of similar status with each other. The assumption was that intellect was genetically determined. However, this desire to match "like with like" became more complicated in 1945, when approximately four million mothers in the United States surrendered newborn babies to adoption, in what's known as the Baby Scoop Era. In her book, *Wake Up Little Susie*, Rickie Solinger said,

> For white girls and women illegitimately pregnant in the pre-Roe era, the main chance for attaining home and marriage . . . rested on the

aspect of their rehabilitation that required relinquishment . . . acting in effect as breeders for white, adoptive parents, for whom they supplied up to nearly 90 percent of all nonrelative infants by the mid-1960s. . . . And the will, veiled though it often was, called for unwed mothers to acknowledge their shame and guilt, repent, and rededicate themselves.[4]

The Child Study for these children would typically say, in a few simple words: "The birth mother is unmarried and cannot provide a home for the child."[5] This solution to move the offspring of unwed middle-class women to middle-class families didn't apply to Black mothers. They were viewed as hypersexual and uncontrollable. Black communities rallied by relying on long-held traditions of informal adoptions, taking care of each other's kin instead of looking at formal adoptions.

The US Children's Bureau began including race in its reporting system in 1948, and thus, the first recorded transracial adoption occurred in 1948.[6] In the early 1950s different strategies began to appear in an attempt to break the implicit adoption color barrier. The Children's Home Society of Minnesota created the "Parents to Adopt Minority Youngsters" campaign and the Boys and Girls Aid Society of Oregon created "Operation Brown Baby"—both to encourage people to consider transracial adoptions. At that time, adoption agencies like these labeled nonwhite adoptions as "special needs" and Black children as "hard to place." The roots of racism in the United States run deep, and perhaps nowhere is this shown more starkly than in the next stage of the history of transracial adoption. Eventually, the Blank Slate theory would extend to race. It became acceptable to adopt a Black or Brown child into a white family, essentially because it was believed that these children would take on all the good characteristics bestowed on them by their white adoptive family. And while this seemingly "color-blind" philosophy was intended to be a positive step away from discrimination based on race, it also opened up a whole new realm of racial complication: Black children adopted into white families were losing their connection to Black culture and family in a very segregated country.

This was most profoundly articulated by the National Association of Black Social Workers, who called transracial adoption "racial genocide" in a 1972 position paper, saying they had taken a "vehement stand against the placement of black children in white homes for any reason."[7] The writers stated that white families would not be able to teach Black children how to deal with racism and that transracial adoptions were done with the benefit of the white family in mind, rather than the benefit of the Black child.

My parents did not know much about any of this in 1982 when they adopted their first child. They tended to adopt another child every couple years until the early 1990s. During this time, successful transracial adoptions were considered news and were reported as human interest stories in newspapers. To many people who encountered us in the grocery store or at the park, our family, white parents and at least eight children in varying shades of white and brown, was confirmation of a post-racial society. Our transracial family was seen as the visible antidote to America's embarrassing disease of racism.

"And isn't it nice that adoptions now happen in a post-racial world?" I joke to the audience and am met with head shakes and rueful laughter. As expected, these folks have done their homework, or have experienced the complexities of racism in transracial adoption themselves and are already a few steps ahead of me. "No," I confirm, just to be sure no one missed the sarcasm. "When it comes to race and adoption, there is so much work still to do."

I let the heavy silence fill the air for a moment, slowly counting to five to let that sink in. Then I click the remote and my Child Study appears on the screen.

CHILD STUDY—Part I: *Adoption Flyer*

Angela is an 11-month-old, black baby girl who has the potential for being very intelligent. However, she will need to be in a home where her parents are committed to a lifetime of treatment and specialized care. She needs a family who is willing to take the chances which come with her uncertain future. She has a severe form of cerebral palsy, known as spastic quadriplegia, her lungs are incredibly weak, her feet are turned upside down and the doctors are fairly certain that she'll never walk. Her new parents must be able to continue with the prescribed physical therapy program so that her physical limitations are minimized as much as possible. We can only guess that this prognosis is a result of her birth mother's drug and alcohol abuses when she was in-utero. It is the assessment of this worker that we move forward by encouraging her biological mother to terminate her parental rights so that she can be adopted. The birth mother desires that her child receive financial benefits that she would not be able to bestow on the child herself.[8]

I speak about the circumstances of my birth and first year of life. Every time I do this, I feel a bit as if I'm outside myself, looking down on my history and cataloging it like a lepidopterist with pins.

At first glance, my Child Study is unremarkable. It totals nine pages of typewritten text broken up in three parts—Part 1: Medical Report; Part 2: Biological Family History; and Part 3: Diet and Nap Schedule. The year 1986 is stamped on the tattered edge of the top right corner. Part 1 includes the adoption flyer that was mailed to children and family services offices throughout the country in an effort to find my new adoptive parents. Part 2 provides vague information about my biological family, and part 3 includes notes from my foster family about my daily routine. There are large swaths of sections that are whited out or redacted. These are to hide any identifying information the law doesn't allow me to know. Precious information, like my birth mother's full name.

In my first job, as a caseworker at an adoption agency, I kept my Child Study nearby at all times. Holding its well-worn pages in my hands filled me with a complex mix of emotions. I'd reread the familiar words and find myself wondering who wrote it and why they used certain language. Sometimes anger would rise in me, an emotion I'd long trained myself to control, especially since my life was wonderfully rich and full. Perhaps my anger stemmed from the way this handful of sentences reduced my baby self to a list of limitations, almost like an advertisement for Imperfect Foods, the grocery delivery service that advertises it services by saying: "Some of our groceries have cosmetic quirks, irregular sizes or are just surplus, which means they used to go to waste or get undervalued. While they may look different than what you'd find in a store, they're sustainable, delicious and high-quality!"[9] Perhaps the anger came from what I knew now but wasn't known then: that not only would I learn to walk but that I'd become a collegiate basketball player. Perhaps I was angry that these Child Study–type documents are still common within the adoption industry, and they continue to be laden with notes that often tell us more about the implicit biases of the writer and the archaic child welfare laws than about the child in need of a home.

My Child Study both inspires me and enrages me. It reminds me why I've chosen to dedicate my life and career to adoption—mentoring adoptees, working with adoptive families and birth families, and studying and advocating for justice in adoption—because I know that I needed more than our society was set up to provide. This Child Study did more than shape my career path. It decided the direction of my entire life.

Although I spent the first thirteen months of my life with my foster family, all of my conscious memories began after I was adopted. In every way most people can imagine, my life was good. People often told me that life with my adopted family was "better" than the life I would have had with my birth family. In certain measurable ways and through the lens of capitalism, this is likely true. Being adopted provided access to healthcare and higher earning income. Thankfully, when this was stated within earshot of my mom, she gave a welcome retort. She'd say, "Well, I don't know about *better*, but her life certainly would've been different." I appreciate this matter-of-fact truth, because it is all we can truly know without a magic crystal ball. What sometimes gets forgotten or glossed over is the essential detail that I had to say goodbye to my biological family before even being given the opportunity to say hello. It meant that my birth culture was wiped away and my roots were effectively severed. But, as strangers often reminded me, I should be grateful for being adopted!

I was severed from two Black families who both had deep roots in Tennessee and was relocated to Bellingham, Washington, smack-dab between Seattle and Vancouver, Canada, where the air is clean and the picturesque snow-capped Mount Baker begs skiers and snowboarders to play hooky from work. Canoeists and kayakers race across the many lakes, and birders watch the herons and eagles soaring overhead. The natural beauty of the city is simply stunning. And its people are just as lovely. But for all of its natural beauty and its embrace of being known as a liberal enclave, it wouldn't be an American city without racism and exclusionary rules; Bellingham was a sundown town. In the 1940s, the rules were simple. Black people were not to be seen come nightfall. They could be in the city during the day, but they had to be gone by sundown. Sundowning was the informal way to keep segregation alive, and these cities were found all over the United States.[10] As a result of this legal segregation, I had mostly white classmates. White doctors. White coaches and mostly white teachers. Many of them were blissfully unaware of the racist history, and warmly welcomed my siblings and me. I always felt like I stood out in our town. But not purely because of my race. Bellingham is nicknamed "the city of subdued excitement." The motto perfectly suits my parents. My mom's calm, frugal, careful approach to life and my dad's tendency to never float his accomplishments. But that was never me. My excitability level is high. I never drink caffeine but jump out of bed each morning with ease. If I could, I'd celebrate every small feat with a new outfit, complete with heels and lipstick to match. In middle school and high school, my flare for fashion didn't fit with the other girls; my neon ensembles, a stark contrast to the uniform everyone else wore in the Pacific Northwest (a black North Face fleece pullover). Two of my sisters, who were adopted when they were teenagers, received an undeniable introduction to the differences between their life as Black girls in the South and their new life with us in Bellingham. Having been used to seeing congregants wearing matching, pressed, pastel-colored suits to their previous church in Kentucky, they turned to each and asked, "Is this church?" upon seeing everyone at Catholic mass wearing T-shirts, jeans, or a casual dress. We were the only Black people in the church.

In an effort to help quell my active brain, my parents encouraged me to journal about my observations. In one entry, dated January 8, 1994, I wrote: *People always tell me I'm so lucky. Is that because no one else wanted me? Did I win the lottery of parents?* I thought about the words used in conjunction with my adoption. Many of those questions resurfaced during my tenure at the adoption agency where I worked after completing my undergraduate degree. "Feelings of not being wanted, fears of being seen as ungrateful, confusion about where I belong—these feelings have followed me my whole life," I tell the audience as I conclude my talk. "For many adoptees, these are lifelong questions, and it's a lifelong journey to find the answers. I am on this journey, both in the micro and macro sense. Both for my personal healing and for the future of the adoption industry. I don't have all the answers—but I know where the answers can be found; in the real-life experiences of adoptees. I invite you to notice the ways the adoption industry currently centers adoptive parents' thoughts and feelings, and to instead pivot toward centering adoptees and their voices."

The hot lights and applause fade behind me into the cool darkness of backstage and I take a deep breath. Just a year prior, I ended a forum with a similar message after *Closure*, the documentary that follows my search for my biological parents, was screened to a sold-out movie theater. During that event, I shared vulnerably about how meeting my birth family helped me reclaim my culture and integrate my racial identity. After the talkback ended, I noticed that my parents were surrounded by strangers who were hugging them and crying. My parents later told me that everyone was very concerned that my movie and the search for my birth parents hurt their feelings.

"They told us that you didn't seem grateful for all that we did, and they wanted us to know that they were grateful for us," my mom told me, while chuckling at the absurdity, adding, "I'm really proud of you for what you said up there."

Backstage, I take a few minutes to compose myself. I know what's to come: the meet and greet. This part is always a little complicated. It's usually a funny mix of flattery (*Your story has completely changed how I parent my adopted son—thank you!*), some frustration (*I've followed you for years and just don't get what all the fuss is about Black and white—we're all one race: the human race!*), and sheer exhaustion as my tired feet and voice long for the solitude and rest of the comfy hotel room bed, a live Golden State Warriors basketball game, and a cup of hot chamomile tea.

But today's meet and greet takes a painful and surprising turn.

"You are my worst fear realized," a Black woman—and total stranger— says, stepping up to the front of the line. As I blink back my shock, she continues, "I came to hear you speak, and you have confirmed my worst fears. You aren't a true Black person." I had noticed her earlier, while speaking on stage. Her large silvery Afro and snazzy pantsuit caught my eye, leading me to a fleeting moment of longing for a Black woman of her age and stature to become a mentor to me.

As I would later learn, I was speaking to a former member of the National Association of Black Social Workers, one of the authors of a scathing rebuke of transracial adoption. The document asserted that white families should not be allowed to adopt Black children for any reason and boldly labeled transracial adoption as "unnatural," "artificial," "unnecessary," and proof that African Americans continued to be assigned to "chattel status."[11] I found the clarity of the statement to be a powerful reclamation of Blackness.

Never breaking eye contact, she continues, "I'm sorry the system erased you from our culture." Her body language communicates defeat. I imagine that she poured much of her career into preserving Black families, and hearing my story was a giant slap in the face. I can only guess, though, because after uttering a few more harsh words, without waiting for my response, she is gone.

I'm flabbergasted, struck numb and, mostly, surprised that her words have such power to hurt me after all the years I've spent coming to embrace my own unique Blackness and supporting other transracial adoptees in their racial identity process. I'd also begun to idolize her. Even with just a glance, seeing her proudly wearing a gray Afro transported me to desiring a friendship. That longing was a surefire repercussion of the lack of Black women in my life. It takes every ounce of composure in my body to look to the next person in line and proceed with the meet and greet with grace and humility, behaving as though the core of my being hadn't just been sliced open. Later, it will all be released in an emotional call with my husband and debriefing with my therapist and trusted transracially adopted friends.

For now, though, as I've done countless times in my life, I suppress my true feelings and soldier on. I've mastered the illusion of appearing invincible. Underneath the feigned invincibility though, a torrent of thoughts are released. I think of the adopted youth I mentor weekly, many of them Black and adopted into white families. I wonder if anyone has ever said anything like that to them. Have I done enough role-playing of ways to respond to microaggressions (like being called an "Oreo")? Have I prepared them for the ways Black folks may view us? Which prompts me to think about my appearance on *Red Table Talk*, a popular talk show, hosted by Jada Pinkett Smith. I was invited to talk about transracial adoption and the impact of cultural erasure. I shared how the mirror used to play tricks on me when I'd look at myself and be surprised to see a Black woman looking back at me. Adrienne "Gammy" Norris told me to "counsel myself," in order to someday find that sense of belonging within the Black community. I was already penning the opening lines of an essay detailing this experience; perhaps I could write something that would offer hope and solidarity to other Black adoptees raised in white homes. And through all of these thoughts, I'm aware that I am deflecting.

I think it's safe to say that my tendency to take my own pain, confusion, and struggle and use it to help others is a coping mechanism that is okay for me to hold onto, so long as I can remain aware of its origins. In mentoring adopted youth, I am saying to them what my own still-healing teenage self needed to hear. In helping birth parents and adopted parents meet and come to know each other, I'm helping build relationships I was not legally allowed to have when I was younger and so longed for. And in advocating for changes to unjust adoption laws that favor parents over adoptees and infantilize adoptees well into their adulthood, I am pushing for a legal system that should have been available to me.

So today, I pack up my hurt along with my laptop and head back to the hotel, ready to take this new twist of pain and hopefully turn it into fuel for a more just adoption system that centers adoptees.

CHAPTER 2

THE ADOPTEE LOUNGE

AFTER ROUTINELY SEEING the lopsided racial equation, with lots of white parents wanting to adopt and all available kids being Black or Brown, I began to wonder if the ways racism has become entangled with foster care and adoption could ever be unwound. I worried that, like the person who wrote my Child Study, I, too, was "encouraging" women to terminate their parental rights without enough information, and I wondered if I'd be able to stand up to the pressures of money and the pervasive feelings of entitlement by prospective adopters in order to advocate for children who entered the world much like I had. I realized that I was perpetuating some of the problematic issues that angered me so much. I watched as new, unhoused mothers were persuaded and even coerced to place their child for adoption. I saw children who had been adopted and who desperately needed to be placed in safe, permanent homes returned after the new parents felt that the child didn't match their advertisement. Child-matching events, sometimes dubbed "KidsFest," were often used to find a home for children. These events brought together young kids who needed to be adopted with parents who were seeking to adopt. The kids would play on the playground while being watched by these parents, some of whom would gingerly go up to a child and interact, assessing whether they'd be a good match for their family. Younger children would be matched with families based on a limited amount of information provided by the biological parents. Although we cannot predict how a biological child may turn out, there was an expectation that these kids would behave as described. I was sickened when I'd see these same kids just years later on Second Chance

Adoptions, a rehoming Facebook site. "Jonny recently turned 8. He needs to be readopted into a family who has no other children younger than 10 and is able to accommodate his needs better. He does not function well as an older sibling; he definitely needs to be the youngest in his new home." The US Department of Health and Human Services estimates that of the approximately 135,000 adoptions finalized every year in the United States, between 1 percent and 5 percent of them end up being legally dissolved.[1] I also noticed that problems within wealthy zip codes (predominantly white neighborhoods) were viewed as private matters to be dealt with behind closed doors, whereas problems in poorer zip codes (predominantly Black neighborhoods) got catapulted into the public child welfare system and oftentimes children were immediately removed from the home. For example, a white father struggling with alcohol addiction in Redmond, Washington (the city where Microsoft is headquartered), might be provided pamphlets and information about Alcoholics Anonymous groups, but when a Black father in Tukwila (a city with the highest percentage of Black people in Washington State) was struggling to remain sober, child protective services was called, and the child was placed in foster care. And even when an adoption seemed to be the best option for a child, I watched as the legal adoption proceedings erased the child's identity by redacting information about their history or expunged any trace of the biological family by providing false information on the birth certificate. No matter how different their circumstances, all of these children were overtly or subliminally told that if they got adopted, they should be grateful because it meant they escaped a life of strife or crime.

After leaving the adoption agency, I began consulting with other adoption agencies and the media to ensure the stories that include adoptees are told with veracity. I started working with birth families and adoptive families, encouraging them to meet and build relationships and helping shepherd those early, awkward meetings. Each step I took deeper into this work left me even more convinced that we must change our approach to adoption, particularly transracial adoption, and that those changes must be influenced by adoptees themselves.

On a stereotypically gray and rainy day in Seattle, I sit with seven adoptees in their private middle school that serves girls and gender nonconforming students. Three are adopted internationally from Haiti, Ethiopia, and China; two are Black and were adopted from foster care; and the other two are white and were adopted privately as newborn babies. Speaking matter-of-factly, I begin the Adoptee Lounge, my monthly mentorship circle for adoptees, by saying "Everything that is shared here stays here. I will not share anything with your parents unless you threaten to hurt yourself or someone else." I open with this standard mandatory reporting statement every session because sadly self-harm is a serious issue for adoptees. The American Academy of Pediatrics conducted a study in 2013 that found that one in four adoptees who seek therapy attempt suicide.[2] The Adoptee Lounges are a space for them to share their stories, to say the quiet things out loud. I am also seeking to help them healthily individuate from their parents. Increasing their autonomy and understanding their layered identities are uniquely important for adoptees so they can live in a compassionate space with others who don't already know them. I ask the children to introduce themselves by sharing how they feel about adoption *today*. The word "today" is key. I emphasize it in order to remind them that their feelings about their own adoption are not static and that it's quite reasonable if they change from day to day. I provide an example, sharing that for some adoptees their birthdays aren't fun because they are reminders that they can't answer simple questions, like what time they were born. Everyone nods, indicating they understand. Ashton, a thirteen-year-old Haitian adoptee, has been playing on her laptop throughout my introductory spiel. She volunteers to go first and turns her laptop around so the screen shows a framed art print with swirly font that reads:

Not flesh of my flesh,
nor bone of my bone,
but still miraculously my own.
Never forget,
not for a single minute,
you grew not under my heart,
but in it.

"This is framed on the wall in my room," Ashton says. "My parents put it there when I was adopted and won't let me take it down. But I kinda don't want it on my wall anymore. That's how I feel about adoption today."

There is a heavy and pensive silence. The middle schoolers look around at each other, which is not unusual during adolescence when identity is being formed, in part, from feedback from their peers. I know their brains are buzzing and their feelings are on the edge of their sleeves, but they don't yet have language to match. I recognize the pensive silence and wonder if we're touching the trifecta—gratitude, confusion, and pain. A sense of gratitude for even having parents at all, intertwined with confusion about growing inside of someone's body, and mired with a difficult-to-describe pain of longing to make sense of it all. They are exhibiting signs of their budding awareness that their parents' beliefs no longer fit with their beliefs. I tread lightly, never desiring to implant my own opinions in their minds, but simultaneously communicating that I understand this dichotomy. I learned how to delve deeper while maintaining sensitivity, kindness, and love from watching the ways my mom responded to microaggressions throughout my childhood.

"Where'd you get those kids?" strangers would ask my mom when we were out running errands.

"My kids entered the world just as we all do. Are you asking if they are adopted?" she'd reply.

"Why didn't her real parents want her?"

"Your question isn't one that we typically discuss with strangers. But she has given me permission to share that she actually has three sets of real parents. Me and my husband, her foster parents, and her birth parents. That's quite something, huh?"

Without fail, grocery store clerks would gush at my parents as we all loaded the food on to the conveyor belt.

"You are a saint for doing what you've done!" I felt the pang of being viewed as a charity case. Even when my mom would diffuse them by replying with something like, "I'm just a regular ol' mom. We wanted to be parents and figured why not parent children who are already born and in need of a home?" Strangers usually responded with grace, respect, and gratitude for having gained this new awareness. But the questions kept coming, and it seemed as though we needed to educate everyone in the entire city. My mom's answers always toed the line between educating and maintaining a sense of privacy for us. Her ability to remain calm and the simplicity of her answers was a powerful role modeling for all of us. The way she chose to prioritize education over anger at the absurdity of the comments was very influential for me. She seemed to know that she was subjected to these intrusive comments just a fraction of the number of times that my siblings and I were. It can be especially dangerous for Black people to get angry. Malcolm X, a proponent of nonviolence, spoke about this in 1965, when he said, "Whenever you and I are discussing our problems we need to be very objective, very cool, calm, collected."[3] He said this the night after his home was bombed. And yes, he said it in a very cool, calm, and collected tone, and it was met by people who were surprised that he didn't look angrier in real life. My mother didn't overtly reference the role our race played in how we could respond, but she modeled it nonetheless. Her careful, calm attention to helping us navigate these situations still guides me today in my work with teenage adoptees.

"What would removing the framed poem on your wall do?" I ask Ashton, breaking the prolonged silence and pressing deeper.

She looked at me and replied with an answer that she'd clearly thought about before, "It would send a message to my parents. I know they are just trying to tell me that I'm special, but they forget that the fact that my birth mom left me lets me know that I'm not." The other girls nodded their heads in solidarity, a few even bouncing their knees with anxiety.

"I understand what Ashton is saying," Abeba says as she slumps down in her chair and twirls her hair around her finger. "I want to know why my birth mom couldn't keep me, too. But my parents say that I'm not old enough to know yet. People always tell me how lucky I am to have these parents, but I don't feel lucky. I want to know where I came from."

"Also," Ashton begins, "my parents adopted me because they couldn't have children of their own. It makes me feel like I'm a backup kid."

A second choice.

These nuanced and complicated feelings are not widely known, which leads to the adoptees in my groups thinking that they are the only ones who feel this way. The astronomical amount of courage it takes to speak the truth is due in part to the common depictions of adoption in the media. Amanda Baden is a researcher and a transracial adoptee who was born in Hong Kong and raised by white parents in the United States. In 2014, she wrote,

Typically, people initially gain exposure to the concept of adoption via fairy tales, stories, films, and comments made by families and friends. For example, movies like *Stuart Little* and *The Blind Side* are just a couple examples of films with adoption or orphan themes. These films depict the narrative of adopted or orphaned children who were cared for by adoptive parents (portrayed as either rescuers or villains) but who ultimately sought reunion with their "real" parents. Introducing audiences—especially children—to adoption and its complexities by using these kinds of images begins to form the "knowledge base." . . . Stories or films may alternately promote or pathologize adoptees' and birth parents' decisions or desires to search for birth parents or birth children just as they may encourage or castigate the decision not to search for them, thereby fueling judgments made about how adoptees should respond to the adoption experience.[4]

The prevailing idea of adoption is tidy and neat. It's a simple recipe. A family with extra love and resources meets a child in need of both. What's not to love about this? Ostensibly, this greater opportunity is a good thing for adoptees. But being the adoptee at the center of the adoption can be tricky and may come with a hard truth that is sometimes hidden and silently acknowledged. Some adoptions are subconsciously measured by what the adoptee has the potential to do with the resources the adoptive parents give. Essentially, *Will they turn out well? What do I owe my parents? How do I show them my gratitude? Through success? Through obedience?*

Georgia Tann, the woman who coined the Blank Slate theory, cemented this trope in 1935, when she persuaded a Mississippi family to adopt two children. Tann was a woman who despised poverty and made a career out of stealing babies from poor people and selling them to wealthy couples. A follow-up report about the status of the two children stated, "The [birth] mother was from an 'ordinary,' poor family. The children were sweet, attractive in appearance. The girl now has a degree in music. The boy has finished his law degree and begun his practice. Each was given an opportunity—and made the most of it."[5] *The Chosen Baby*, a landmark children's book published in 1939, also helped to cement the rags-to-riches paradigm. The author said, "The Chosen Baby is intended for parents of young children, who wish to make the first explanation of adoption as happy as it is true."[6] The book preached a similar message to the poem on Ashton's wall. It emphasized that adoptees should feel special because they were chosen.

What complicated matters for me and stunted my courage to rebuke strangers who pleaded that I show more gratitude for my adoption was the weightiness of the confession (I wish I wasn't adopted) and the impossibility of explaining that it both is and isn't as serious as it sounds. So instead, I acquiesced to the relentless pleas and learned that to speak honestly about adoption is to hurt someone. And it's to risk being misperceived.

In the Adoptee Lounge, we can utter seeming contradictions, like one I've wrestled with my entire life: I love my adoptive parents. And I wish I wasn't adopted.

CHAPTER 3

HOW MUCH DID I COST?

A DDY WAS NINE when I first began mentoring her. I was twenty-six. She wrote to me through her parents' email, saying,

> I really want to talk to you because you are kinda like me. You are Brown and grew up with white parents. And you were adopted from foster care. I want to know if you can help me find out how much I costed. I've asked my parents, but my parents don't exactly tell me. Do you know how much you costed? Do you think we were the same price?

Addy and I met at her home on a rainy October day in Seattle. "My favorite animals are the oxpecker and the rhino," Addy began before I'd even sat down. "I love them together because they have a symbiotic relationship. The oxpecker feeds off the rhino's back, eating the little insects that are making the rhino itchy. I love how they help each other, even though they aren't even in the same family and look nothing alike! This is kinda like my family. None of us look like each other, but we still help each other out."

At twenty-six years old, I wasn't accustomed to conversations with nine-year-olds about the correlation between animal symbiosis and adoption, much less while preparing to make friendship bracelets at her kitchen counter.

Addy's parents had told me that their daughter was viewed as a good student at school but also as a bully. I experienced this shortly after we began our session, when she rolled her eyes at me after I admitted that I didn't know much about oxpeckers or rhinos. She lectured me in an exasperated tone, before continuing her story, describing the ways in which she is similar to the oxpecker.

"I'm Brown, and I feel like I'm always just picking invisible scabs off my parents." She told me about how oxpeckers are mainly thought of as parasites because they feed on the blood of the rhinos, and when they suck the blood of the rhino, they make new scabs that will get infected with new parasites. "I feed off my parents. Like, they give me everything I need to stay alive, but it seems like sometimes I also am infecting them with new scabs."

I was admittedly dumbfounded by the impressive analogy. Addy's self-knowledge (and animal knowledge!) impressed me, but I sensed there was more going on than the matter-of-fact animal kingdom comparison she was sharing. I dug a bit deeper and asked why she'd consider the oxpecker her favorite animal after all she'd told me about how irritating it is to the rhino. "Well, I have to love being adopted, right?"

I had wondered if Addy had been speaking about a fictionalized oxpecker or herself. My hunch was satiated when she switched to using the word "I." The way Addy was transferring the negative qualities she felt about herself to the animal is called projection. It's a defense mechanism. And one that many adoptees, including myself, can relate to. Sometimes it's easier to talk about nonhuman objects than about ourselves and our parents.

"Did you know that elephants, waterbucks, and hartebeests do not tolerate oxpeckers?" Addy went on and I felt certain we were heading toward the heart of her concerns. "I know that some families would never have adopted me because my skin is too dark." Addy's voice was so soft I had to lean in slightly to hear. "But, I guess being adopted is good, even if it means that I'm kinda like a guest in the family. If the oxpeckers didn't have the rhinoceros, they'd be dead."

We sat in silence for a moment as we both pondered the weight of what Addy had just shared. When mentoring sessions reach a pinnacle moment, if appropriate, I sometimes interject an opportunity for laughter. So I took this opportunity to have a laugh with Addy.

"I may not know much about oxpeckers, but I do love birds. So I have a question for you: Why didn't the eagles like to talk to the press?"

Addy looked at me quizzically.

"They think they are a bunch of vultures."

Addy wasn't going to give me the pleasure of seeing her belly laugh, but she did give me a fist bump and whispered, "That was pretty good." Together we placed one brightly colored string over another, braiding our bracelets while sitting in comfortable, shared silence. I allowed my brain to marvel at Addy's deep insight and how she was already hitting on some of the deepest and most difficult issues related to transracial adoptions. Many adult adoptees barely know how to name the uncertainty of belonging within an adopted family, let alone turning it into a sub-Saharan metaphor. Even in loving families like Addy's, adoptees can sometimes feel like "guests" or "outsiders"; they may feel an ongoing obligation to be constantly grateful to their adoptive parents, and, of particular significance for Addy and me, they may view Black babies as less desirable for adoption than white babies.

Addy was unfortunately right. White babies have a higher market value than Brown-skinned children. In 2010, researchers at the Centre for Economic Policy Research found that a non-Black baby is seven times more likely to "attract the interest and attention of potential adoptive parents than an African-American baby."[1] The researchers obtained data from AdoptUSKids, an adoption organization that operates similarly to Zillow for home buying. AdoptUSKids and other adoption photo-listing websites allow potential adoptive parents to filter the attributes of adoptable children by race, gender, and the cost of finalizing the adoption.[2] Researchers examined that data to see which children, by race, were of greatest interest to prospective adoptive parents.

This question of cost is uncomfortably wrapped in layers of emotion and periods in history when we've exchanged money for humans, including days when slave traders promised fit and ripe bodies for their buyers. The racial parallels between those days and today are not lost on transracial adoptees, even someone as young as Addy. Making these connections about the losses and gains of adoption is scary. And Addy was diving deep at a young age. This process, popularly termed "coming out of the fog," is a bit terrifying at any age. Sara Easterly, an adult adoptee, illuminates this during a conversation on a podcast. She says,

> It's particularly hard for adoptees to look honestly at adoption when we're children. We have so much emotion and it's just too much emotion for consciousness. And in many cases, it's pre-verbal experience. I didn't want to face the fact that babies were precious. There was a story I had told myself that I wasn't precious enough to keep. It was easier just to kind of say, oh, babies aren't anything special—than to actually realize I was one of those too, and I actually was special.[3]

Addy and I share the trait of having an insatiable curiosity for truth and a hopeful desire for a contented spirit. Being a couple decades older than Addy, I knew that lies, omissions, or simply not knowing our full story cannot coexist with contentedness. I knew Addy's quest was just beginning, and I was grateful that I could journey with her a bit, sharing some of the struggle and resulting wisdom of my own path.

. . . .

When I was a kid, strangers would occasionally offer unsolicited information to my parents when I was within earshot. They'd look at our family and say, "We might adopt too, after we have our own kids and after we've saved up a bit of money." In a strange effort to encourage random strangers to think about adopting, I began to offer myself as a test case to prove adoption was affordable. That *I* was affordable. "Well, my parents were given a discount because I had special needs. So, maybe don't assume it's out of your price range," I'd say. It wasn't an enticing sell, apparently; in those days I doubt I talked anyone into it. But it was true: my cost was written in the flyer sent to my parents:

> Our fee for Angela would normally be $5000, but since she has special needs, we'll lower the price. We'll also take into account your current income, and the number of adopted kids already in your home. We will invoice you $1500 but would be glad to receive $1000. Let me know if you'd like to negotiate this further.

In truth, my "special needs" diagnosis was probably as much about my race as about the medical challenges the doctors anticipated for me. The term "special needs" is used in adoption paperwork to describe any child for whom the agencies have a hard time finding an adoptive home. It's heartbreaking and infuriating but, by this definition, almost every child of color in the foster system is labeled special needs.

My personal disabilities did not turn out to be lifelong and debilitating like the doctors predicted. When I began to pull myself up to try to walk, my foot remained turned upward and my limbs remained stiffened. With consistent physical therapy and to the shock of the doctors, my foot eventually turned downward, and I was walking and running before I was four years old. But it wouldn't be until I was five years old that I was first fitted with hearing aids. My foster parents were focused on my physical mobility, taking weekly trips to physical therapy sessions, performing daily at-home exercises, and rotating my hips and stretching out my legs just to be able to change my diaper. So they didn't notice that I wasn't startled at loud noises and didn't begin babbling or talking. My mom noticed I wasn't responding to my name, and so, when I was four years old, we headed into the pediatrician for a hearing screening. However, even though I'd failed the hearing test one year prior, the doctor was impressed by my ability to speak and thought the results of the hearing test must have been a fluke.

Once I got hearing aids, I caught up quickly, marveling at the sound of birds chirping and other sounds I'd not known existed and soon speaking without any impediments. However, the humiliation factor at school was high. I didn't want to wear devices that my friends' grandparents wore. I'd grown tired of my peers at Silver Beach Elementary school asking me about the strange looking tube that was connected to a goofy shade of "skin tone" brown wax that contoured to my inner ear. When I was seven, I came up with a great plan to hide them. I kept my left hearing aid in but wore my chemically straightened hair in a side ponytail to cover up my left ear. I removed my right hearing aid and stuck it underneath the entry mat on my way out the front door. Not too bad of a plan for a little kid! Except that by that evening, my right hearing aid had been crunched into many pieces under the door mat and, when my mom found it, I was in big trouble.

Throughout my childhood, my parents taught us to see ourselves as complete human beings and demonstrated to us how to not let anyone make us feel small. My older sister was born premature, weighing just one pound, fourteen ounces at birth. In adopting her, my parents became fluent in all things related to wheelchairs, crutches, assistive-technology devices, and anything else necessary to help her navigate the world. Cerebral palsy is actually the least interesting thing about her, yet it always seemed to attract the most attention. "What happened to her?" strangers would ask, looking over the top of my sister's head and directing their question to my mom. "Well," my mom would reply, "she's right here if you'd like to ask her." I loved how my mom oh-so-gently reminded them that an inability to walk does not mean that she was also unable to think or speak for herself.

Sometimes, though, we'd prefer the strangers talk to our parents instead of us. Being overlooked was easier than having them gush, "Your parents are saints!" while they watched my mom corral all of us into the van, then fold up my sister's wheelchair and hoist it into the trunk. "I could never do that," they'd say. Then to my siblings and me: "You must be so grateful!" *What did they mean by that? They could never adopt? They could never adopt kids with disabilities? They could never love someone who doesn't look like them? Did they see us as charity cases? Kids to be pitied? Representations of the consequences of bad choices?*

In 2013, journalist Michele Norris hosted NPR's Race Card Project, an initiative that invited people to submit six-word sentences related to race. One participant wrote, "Black Babies Cost Less To Adopt." Fee structures were in place in an effort to disguise this distasteful reality, attempting to blur the capitalist lines that labeled light-skinned babies more valuable than others. Given this, it was hard to remember that nearly two centuries ago even white babies weren't desirable. This was due in part to how orphaned children were spoken of—"street Arabs" or "guttersnipes"—but also because the assumption was that poor and uneducated women gave birth to genetically flawed children. They implemented a sliding scale, but the facts remained. I remember a fee structure document where white and biracial babies "cost" upward of $30,000, while an unborn Black girl was $18,000.

The question of "how much I cost," and the need adoptees have to get an answer, seems to represent several underlying assumptions about ownership, family, belonging, and identity. Feelings of ownership are baked into our society's understanding of relationships, where the notion of love is very much tied to an idea of exclusive possession, exclusive trust, and exclusive loyalty. In 1998, a *Vanity Fair* writer joked that Chinese baby girls were "the season's hot accessory in the Hamptons." While it might have gotten laughs to compare adopted children to the cute spring line of purses, the pain and confusion of feeling like that purse—purchased for a certain price—is a daily reality for adoptees.

Ultimately, pondering "how much I cost" leads many adoptees to question the situations of their birth families and the situations—often involving lack of money—that led to their being placed for adoption. "My adoptive caregivers flat out told me they adopted internationally because it was cheaper," one adoptee shared. "The money they used to buy me would have changed my mother's life and given her the resources to keep me." Another adult adoptee told me, "My parents never disclosed the money aspect, talking about money and my cost always felt dirty. I feel that agencies, facilitators, and lawyers in a lot of cases are charging so much and yet not using the funds to help the expectant moms. I wish some of the money went to give the birth moms some counseling."

After finishing up our friendship bracelets and tying them on each other's wrists, Addy and I moved to her room where I taught her the word "exulansis," as a balm for this world, which both she and I viewed as chaotic and nonsensical. Exulansis comes from John Koenig's book *The Dictionary of Obscure Sorrows*, in which he has coined and defined words for emotions that are currently indescribable. Exulansis is defined as "the tendency to give up trying to talk about an experience because people are unable to relate to it."[4] Just like me, Addy latched onto this word right away, as it describes our ongoing experience of trying to explain our complex internal landscape to people who struggle to understand. In defining it, though, we also both found strength—a way to keep pushing for our voices and experiences to be heard, even in a world that doesn't get it.

In the privacy of Addy's purple and blue bedroom, we practiced not giving up when trying to explain the seemingly unexplainable.

"How would you respond when someone says, 'Wow! You're adopted? That's so cool! Tell me your story'?" I asked.

Addy averted her eyes and sighed with discomfort, even though we were just practicing. I got it.

This simple question can be dreadfully heavy for adoptees. I often squirm when I'm asked to "tell my story," because the pressure to produce a coherent, inspiring narrative is thick. It's exulansis. In elementary school, my favorite teacher would say, "Wow, it's so incredible that you are so healthy. Without your parents you probably wouldn't be here right now!" At that time, I would say, "Yeah, you're probably right," and would dutifully recount details about my adoption that confirmed her statement. "I doubt I would've learned to walk, and my birth parents probably couldn't have afforded hearing aids for me!" In telling this version of my story, I overrode my own experience and perception of my life in favor of what would make my teacher feel most comfortable. "My birth mother was unhealthy and unstable," I'd say. "She couldn't possibly have given me a good home, so I got a better one. I was one of the lucky ones."

Like I did as a kid, adoptees often answer these questions by reflexively spouting off the chronology of our lives as we've heard others describe it. Answers are often a regurgitation of what their adoptive parents have said about their adoption. I heard one adult adoptee respond to the request to "tell her story" by saying, "I was left under a bridge in Guatemala when I was a baby. Thankfully, someone found me and brought me to an orphanage. My parents brought me home when I was two years old. I was severely malnourished and supposedly wasn't held by anyone for weeks on end. Miraculously, I'm totally attached to my parents. Usually, people like me suffer from attachment disorder."

Another adult adoptee said, "My parents adopted me after struggling with infertility for three years. I was their miracle baby. My birth mother chose them to adopt me two days after they miscarried."

These answers are not ideal because they are quasi-fictional accounts that are based on our adoptive parents' memories and feelings. They aren't our truths or our birth families' truths—they are our adoptive parents' recounting of the moment.

"It [being adopted] is actually not that cool," Addy said. But she looked up at me with fear in her eyes and added, "I could never just say that though. People would think I was not grateful—even my own parents might feel that way!"

I smiled and nodded. I reassured Addy that this fear is normal and it's okay to worry how her adoptive parents would feel if she were more honest. I shared with her a couple of lines from my Adoptee Manifesto. It's okay to feel two things at once, you can be grateful to your adoptive parents and also wish you weren't adopted. You can love your adoptive family deeply and still want to know your birth family. You can be simultaneously happy and sad about your adoption. "I still feel that way most days, Addy," I admitted. Her eyes widened with amazement as she inched closer to me.

After a minute I told her I really liked her answer, that adoption isn't actually all that cool. Giving her additional permission, I add: "If you feel like you need to tack on another sentence, how about adding, 'That's actually a very sensitive and private question'?" A huge grin burst forth on Addy's face. She has a beautiful smile and it warms something deep in my heart. She seemed to relish the idea that she could stand up to people and let them know they were prying. I think Addy is going to do just fine setting boundaries. I just wish she didn't have to be quite this good at it.

CHAPTER 4

MY GHOST KINGDOM

I LIKE TO IMAGINE I was warm and comfortable for nine months inside Deborah's uterus. I imagine that it was pitch black, but I was comforted by the steady, thrumming, and constant beat of my mother's heart. Here and there sounds may have punctured the comforting rhythm, muffled and distant, filtered through deep layers and gone as fast as they started—but never requiring much attention because the steady beat persisted, wrapping everything up and keeping everything still and safe. During the last trimester, though, I must have learned a lot about the outside environment. I'm guessing I learned that the world outside could be dangerous and toxic. I must have known this because of the stress hormones that made up my environment. And then suddenly there were bright lights and new sensations all around me. The biochemistry I'd waded through and loved suddenly vanished. I was passed around from a nurse to a social worker, then to a foster family, and finally to an adoptive family. I was passed around in search of a healthier life. This was a startling beginning to life. I call it a postnatal culture shock.

What happened to my mother? Where did she go?

Most of the losses we experience in life require little explanation and are universally recognized. A loved one was among us—and then they weren't. They were breathing and now they aren't. We assemble a ceremony or ritual to mark the loss. We miss them, mourn for them, and are comforted by others who understand and may grieve with us. Over time, the sadness over their absence, while it may never evaporate, dissipates. But some loss is less clear, even more distressing, and may last forever. It's ambiguous. That's the kind of ceremony I had.

Author and researcher Pauline Boss defines two types of ambiguous loss. One arises when there is a physical presence but a psychological absence—for example, when a loved one has dementia or is emotionally unavailable. The other type, conversely, emerges when there's a psychological presence but a physical absence.[1] This was mine. My birth family was always on my mind but was not physically accessible.

Was my birth mom right-handed or left-handed?

Did my birth father have dimples?

Did either of them have Achoo Syndrome (a dominant trait also called photo sneeze reflex), or "hand clasping" (learning which thumb one automatically places on top of the other when clasping hands together)?

When did she learn how to drive?

Is my hearing loss genetic?

Did she look back at me as she walked out the hospital door?

When she felt me growing inside was it with the dreaded anticipation of weeds overtaking a well-tended garden?

This cyclone of questions about my roots permeated my brain and undergirded the seeming ease with which I floated through life. My white peers marveled at my athleticism and the quick clip for which I racked up track awards and earned a college basketball scholarship. As I stood atop the podium after winning the 400-meter dash, I both beamed with pride as I looked up at my proud parents and wondered internally, *Was my birth mom athletic? Magic Johnson has a huge smile like me and he's super athletic. Maybe he is my birth dad?*

I imagined my birth mom had teeth like mine. Straight, glossy, and unstained. My two front teeth are uniquely large and fit in with the rest of my large smile, which takes up a third of my face. The whiteness of the enamel also garnered a lot of attention. "You have such a beautiful smile!" strangers would say. *My birth mom must've had a million-watt smile, too,* I'd think, disregarding, or perhaps blocking out, the information in part 2 of my Child Study, which stated, "The birthmother is from a deprived background. This was evidenced by her inability to secure employment, her appearance including rotting teeth, tattered clothing[,] and the lower socio-economic neighborhood that she lives in."

Betty Jean Lifton is an adoptee and a psychologist who coined the term "Ghost Kingdom." She defined it as the hypothetical world adoptees enter when imagining their birth relatives.[2] Since nothing is real in this make-believe realm, adoptees can meander through all kinds of fantastical imaginings of what their birth family is like. My Ghost Kingdom was a rich tapestry of wonder. There, my birth parents became grandiose idealized people, like Magic Johnson. My birth mother was the actress Brandy, after I saw her in the 1997 film *Cinderella*; then it was Lisa in the '90s sitcom *Saved by the Bell*. One day my birth mother died in a tragic accident when she was skydiving out of a helicopter and the parachute didn't deploy.

Taking day trips to Seattle increased my exposure to Black people, which led me to wonder if my birth relatives were walking past me in the crowded streets downtown. I stifled my attraction to the few Black boys I knew because of the unfounded fear that I might be related to them. *What if I dated my biological brother?* In my Ghost Kingdom, my birth mother has lived in mansions and shacks, she's been depressed and jubilant. She misses me and then forgets about me. Sometimes, she even wishes she had never put me up for adoption. In my Ghost Kingdom, I imagined that I spent the last trimester in the womb, kicking and trying to be noticed. The extra pounds of fat on my birth mother's tummy successfully hid the growing protrusion of her belly, making it such that she didn't even notice me. This meant that any potential birth father wouldn't have known to think about me either. My Ghost Kingdom was rife with traits that when pieced together always led to a narrative of a woman who survived an untold amount of intergenerational pain.

In her book, Pauline Boss asks, "What happens when a family member or a friend who may be still alive is lost to us nonetheless? . . . These losses are always stressful and often tormenting." Ambiguous losses are the most devastating and traumatizing of losses because sufferers must live with ambiguity that might stay with them throughout their lives. For adoptive families and their relatives and friends, an adoption is cause for celebration. Extended family members and members of the community may not fully appreciate that for adoptees, adoption is directly tied to the ambiguous loss of one's birth family. Boss illustrates her point, quoting from an old English nursery rhyme, with an example certain to resonate with anyone who grieves an absent parent:

As I was walking up the stair,
I met a man who was not there
He was not there again today
Oh, how I wish he'd go away.

I didn't know this nursery rhyme as a child and young adult, but I wish I had, as it perfectly reflects the daily, hourly—and on some boring days—even moment by moment palpable absence I experienced related to my birth parents. No matter what I did or where I went, they were always there and, of course, were not there at all.

My parents were committed to sharing as much of my story with me as they were able. My mom understood the inevitability of human nature, that when faced with the absence of facts we create stories out of thin air. From a young age, my parents showed unconditional support for the way I waded through my Ghost Kingdom. Being able to wonder aloud about my roots conveyed a meaningful message to me. They understood that even though I didn't have enough information to search for my birth parents online, I was still searching for my birth parents. Since my adoption was closed, they didn't have much to share with me beyond the Child Study they had received. As I grew up, I'd ask the same questions and receive the same answers. But with each passing year, my understanding, curiosity, and ability to process increased so even the same, partial information would elicit new responses in me. In my seventh-grade diary, I wrote, "I performed at my piano recital today! Afterwards I talked to my mom about if she thought my birth mom was a pianist. My mom said she didn't know. I still wonder if she's ever performed in Carnegie Hall?"

This entry was proof of not only my search for my roots, but perhaps more importantly, the clear unconditional support that I had from my mom.

Children whose adoptive parents rarely discuss the absent birth parents or birth siblings feel the loss more keenly. In a study of young adult adoptees published in a 2005 issue of the *Journal of Social and Personal Relationships*, sociocultural researchers Kimberly Powell and Tamara Afifi correlate heightened ambiguous loss symptoms with children and youth who lack information about their birth parents and have lived with a family who failed to honor the adoptees' connection with their family or culture of origin.

Occasionally, I receive emails from adoptive parents who triumphantly tell me that their child doesn't ever think about their birth parents, yet in the next sentence they request to set up a mentorship session between their child and me because they've noticed that their child is struggling with anxiety. After conversing with the kids, I often find that they are wallowing in their Ghost Kingdom alone, and this is the source of the anxiety. Their parents don't realize that their child is thinking about their birth parents. Evidence that they are searching for their roots can be seen when they're scanning a big auditorium trying to see if anyone has any features that resemble their own or through comments such as "I wonder how tall I'm going to be when I grow up."

When my birth mother relinquished her parental rights to the state of Tennessee, she also relinquished the opportunity to have a relationship with me or to even know where I ended up. The process is, unfortunately, designed for this outcome, marked by secrets and lies in an attempt to protect birth families and adoptive families. Instead of allies, adoptive parents and birth parents are treated like adversaries. I was not allowed to learn any information about my birth family or the circumstances of my adoption beyond what was written in the Child Study. The document was non-identifying, which meant that any details that could lead me to be able to find my biological family members were redacted.

Legally, these types of documents can include background information about the circumstances of an adoption, the ages of the birth mother and birth father, ethnicity, nationality, educational background, any religious affiliations, descriptions of their appearance, medical histories of birth mothers, and professions and hobbies of the birth parents. This list sounds exhaustive; however, if the social workers did not collect the information, then it wouldn't be included in the Child Study. I can imagine that my birth mother wasn't highly motivated to share all that background information at such a stressful time.

I'm not sure how young I was the first time my parents shared my Child Study with me. I expect my precocious nature and persistence probably led to them sharing it prior to me walking or talking (both feats happened later than a neurotypically developed child). The simple words in the handful of pages became more important to me as I got older. To this day, I read the Child Study yearly. It is worn and tattered. The year 1986 is stamped in different places on each page, and the ink is so worn down it's barely legible. The words mean something different to me each time I read through it, waxing and waning with my maturity level and interests as far back as I can remember.

CHILD STUDY—Part II: *Family History*
Deborah is 31 years old. She has an unkempt gray afro and the discoloration in her face due to years of neglected hygiene and homelessness.

In my young childhood, learning how old my birth mother was when she gave birth to me meant very little. *She was old when she gave birth to me.* That was the extent of my thought process. When I became a teenager, thinking of my birth mother as a thirty-one-year-old made her seem ancient. Thanks to television shows like MTV's *Teen Mom*, I struggled to understand how someone that old wouldn't have been able to keep me.

Aren't teenagers the only people who need to place their children for adoption?

But learning her name was thrilling. The name Deborah became larger than life to me. I'd break out into a large smile anytime I met anyone else with the name. I remember it took on a vaguely royal and biblical meaning, eliciting images of pre-Roman queens. Even at a young age, I knew Deborah wasn't royalty. I didn't fully get it yet, of course, but there was an intrinsic knowing that being poor played a major role in Deborah's life.

In middle school I read that sentence in conjunction with the few sentences after it.

CHILD STUDY—Part II: *Family History*
Deborah is 31 years old. She has an unkempt gray afro and the discoloration in her face due to years of neglected hygiene and homelessness.

I wrote my reflection in my journal: *It's a bummer that Deborah didn't have a home. She should've gotten a job so that she could've kept me.*

My family would periodically volunteer at the Community Meal program hosted by our local Catholic church. Volunteering increased my proximity to houseless individuals, which helped me to build empathy for their plight.

"What's your favorite color?" I asked each person while they came through the food line. One by one they'd look down at me quizzically, caught off guard by the unusual question coming from me, a young girl wearing high-top Nike shoes and a Michael Jordan basketball jersey.

"Blue," one man answered as my mom plopped food down on his tray. *Trustworthy, peaceful, dependable,* I thought, reflecting on what I had learned about the color in a book I'd previously read about color symbolism.

"Red," the next person in line replied. *Fierce, bold,* I thought, recounting the way Toni Morrison used the color red in *Beloved.*

"I have two favorite colors—pink and bright pink," a woman said as my mom dished up her plate.

These interactions were transformative for my development and understanding of the circumstances of my adoption. Volunteering at the soup kitchen was one strategy my parents employed to humanize the unhoused. And it was strategic, because not only did it help me to increase my compassion in general for people experiencing houselessness, but it also humanized my birth mother. Everyone that came through the food line became layered. I recognized that not only were they in difficult circumstances but they likely had hobbies and interests that may have been like mine. They had a backstory to their lives.

If this person is houseless and has a favorite color, then my birth mom probably does too.

I began to shift any blame I'd directed toward Deborah and her inability to care for me away from her personal behavior and onto the root causes of houselessness. I began to understand the instability being houseless causes. I watched people schlep their belongings into the church, only to forget their hat, their hairbrush, or their umbrella on the table. Or sometimes people forgot their medicine. I watched people use the bathrooms to brush their teeth and realized the hardships of keeping good hygiene. In my Ghost Kingdom, I no longer pictured Deborah standing on the street corner with a sign begging for money.

I pictured myself without my home base, my purple bedroom, and the hardwood flooring (which was installed, replacing the carpet to help keep my allergies at bay), my medals and trophies proudly displayed on the shelves (which I was able to participate in because my asthma was controlled), my neatly organized bookshelves (which my mom dusted regularly when I was out of the house to minimize the dust mites in the air), my trove of blankets that I nestled into after my weekly allergy immunotherapy appointments, my nebulizer and the rest of my medicine in the top drawer ready whenever I needed it (insurance covered much of the costs). I began to realize how hard it would be for me to stay healthy without a home. My parents had successfully planted the seeds that my birth mother's "choices" around houselessness or even choosing to place me for adoption were brought on by a myriad of structural causes—causes that I would later come to understand as gentrification, historic disinvestment in communities of color, racial housing inequality, and a gutted social safety net.

In a journal from eighth grade, I wrote my birth mother a letter,

Dear Ms. Deborah,

There are some things I have always wanted to say to you: I think the world of you. I admire your ability to go through with an undesired pregnancy, especially without any help from doctors, books or friends. I am amazed by your courage and that you would keep your pregnancy a secret in order to protect yourself (and me?). I don't know many people who have the strength to walk into the hospital pregnant and alone and walk out alone and without me, your baby. Everyone tells me that I should be grateful that I was put up for adoption, but I don't really think that's fair. I have had a great life, but I think I would've had a great life if I had stayed with you, too.

Thank you for reading,

Oh, and by the way, the social workers named me Angela

By my early twenties rereading the Child Study led to anger at the social worker and writer of this document.
How dare she write in such a judgmental way about my birth mother!

While working at the adoption agency, I quietly began to evaluate whether caseworkers continued to offer personal judgments about pregnant women who were considering adoption. I wondered if we still offered discounts to children who were deemed "hard to place," and if so, how was that discussed? Nearly daily, I'd hear a colleague mention that our job was to do what is in "the best interest of the child." It rolled off the tongue in nearly every meeting, but it seemed to mean something different depending on who was speaking. It is a loaded phrase and a coded phrase. In Regina Kunzel's book *Fallen Women, Problem Girls*, she writes about how midwives of the early twentieth century wanted to redeem unmarried mothers. They viewed them as "a moral problem to be solved by sisterhood."[3] These midwives were committed to keeping mother and child together—a principle Kunzel describes as "the cornerstone of womanly benevolence in maternity homes." However, there was a change in language about unmarried mothers by 1920, when social workers began labeling women as "feebleminded" or "sex delinquents." This implicitly suggested that the unwed mother was beyond reformation while her child was explicitly in danger from her influence. The maternity homes began to view the mother as the villain and positioning the unborn baby as the victim in need of rescue.

I began to think about what I might have said had I been able to speak as a newborn baby. What would I have wanted for my life? Was it the same as what the professionals were advocating for? I suppose I might have asked the professionals to provide Deborah with relief during this time of distress and even before that, when I was in utero. Because by doing that, I would have been relieved of distress, too—in utero, as a newborn, and as a child and adult. The distress in utero might have hindered my brain development, possibly leading to my medical issues. Then there's the distress of being separated from her as a newborn and the future distress of not knowing where I came from and having to spend years investigating and searching for her. And above all, the distress of wondering why Deborah couldn't keep me. Those foundational questions nagged at me at all hours of the day and often turned into nightmares of being abandoned. But no one could read my mind or predict the future. So the caseworkers did the best they could with the information they had at the time, which meant leaving Deborah to fend for herself. Deborah's health didn't come into the discussion when thinking about my best interest, at least not after my birth. I came to this conclusion after sitting in many meetings where I'd try to advocate for the biological parent, for the purpose of that child's health. I'd ask, "Did anyone follow up with the birth mother after she gave birth?" or "Did anyone teach the birth mother how to stop the breast milk from coming in, which may be causing pain?" Those questions were usually met with heavy sighs and remarks about how that was a kind, sensitive thought, but then the actions were redirected to ensuring that the baby had a new adoptive home. My questions seemed to create disjointed meetings that caused us to veer off the scheduled agenda.

· · · · · · · · · ·

Social workers are not meant to be pieces of a well-oiled machine. Humans are much too complicated for that. Social workers are supposed to be subversive and disruptive. However, in 1915, Dr. Abraham Flexner famously contended that social work was not a true profession because it lacked specific application of theoretical knowledge to solving human issues. As a result, the field began concentrating on casework and the scientific method, eroding the sole commitment to social activism.

I remembered Dr. Huberta Jackson-Lowman's essay "Denigration of Black Motherhood," in which she writes, "No respect was demonstrated for the essentiality of the mother-child bond when Afrikan women were kidnapped and enslaved, on the auction block, nor with regard to the day-to-day demands faced by enslaved Afrikan women."[4] I wondered if any social workers showed respect for Deborah and me immediately after I was born. *Did we bond? Did we get any time together? Did anyone advocate for her? For me?* Upon discovering that Deborah was houseless, why wouldn't the adoption agency, hospital staff, or anyone else mobilize to help her find a home and in turn perhaps be able to keep me? After seeing her rotted, abscessed teeth, why didn't the agency connect her with local dental support for low-income people? If they had done this, perhaps her pain level would've decreased, thus allowing for a less stressful pregnancy.

A few months into my tenure at the adoption agency and armed with more knowledge about how little regard my coworkers paid to birth mothers, I reread the first full paragraph in that section.

CHILD STUDY—Part II: *Family History*

Deborah is 31 years old. She has an unkempt gray afro and the discoloration in her face due to years of neglected hygiene and homelessness. Deborah has five siblings. None of them know about this pregnancy. Deborah is currently homeless. She has four other children. Three of the children live nearby but are not in Deborah's custody. One other child was placed for adoption to a family that has stated they aren't interested in adopting Angela.

The sentences about my four biological siblings weighed more heavily in my mind. Most of my Ghost Kingdom was composed of imaginings of my birth mother and father but to realize that I had biological siblings out in the world opened entirely new possibilities of connection.

Could I ever meet them?

Do we look alike?

Would people see us together and say, "Oh, I can see the family resemblance"?

Why wouldn't the other family want to adopt me to stay with one of my biological siblings?

Learning that Deborah had four other children prior to my birth led me to read an arsenal of literature about the connection between poverty, racism, and adoption. I thought about President Johnson's "War on Poverty" in the 1960s and then the Republicans' "War on Drugs" in the 1980s. Overall, both these programs resulted in an increase of private and voluntary organizations to help poor families, less governmental aid for poor people, and an increased use of social control institutions to manage the poor. Between 1986 and 1995, the number of children in foster care increased from 280,000 to nearly 500,000, a 76 percent increase in just nine years.[5] This explosion in children entering foster care was most significantly carried out in Black families. It wasn't until 1993 that Congress created the Family Preservation and Family Support Services Program. Their concern was that states were focusing too little on preventing children from entering foster care or being reunified with their biological families.

It occurred to me that my adoption was likely caught in the crosshairs of these governmental strategies. I began to realize that the matrix that involves the development of punitive policies across several systems penalizes Black mothers and reinforces the state's control over their bodies and, by proxy, mine.

CHAPTER 5

THE SEARCH

J ESSE, A TWELVE-YEAR-OLD GIRL, plays on her phone during most of the Adoptee Lounge. Her peers describe her as a "gamer." I know she's paying attention; fiddling with her phone during the Adoptee Lounge is how she manages overwhelming feelings. I welcome the use of items to fidget with because it gives our restless energy somewhere to go. In other words, it can help to regulate anxiety. Eventually Jesse shares that it bothers her when her parents tell her she was put up for adoption because her birth mom loved her so much. "I was placed for adoption when I was a baby. My parents never even met my birth mom," she notes with sincerity, "so how do they know that she loved me?"

Ouch. I wince. All of the others dart their eyes around, some twisting their fingers together in their laps.

The phrase *put up for adoption* pains me to hear. It was originally used in the 1800s, when 250,000 young children were relocated from New England to the Midwest by way of cattle cars, which became known as "Orphan Trains." Upon reaching each city, the children were *put up* on a stage to sing or dance, hoping to attract the attention of someone who might want them in their family. The children were inspected like they were livestock. Muscles were felt. Teeth were checked. This archaic form of adoption was not how the adoptions of the youths I was working with happened. For them to unknowingly refer to themselves this way made me sad. Speaking this way unwittingly furthers the stigma that adoptees need to prove their worth within a family unit. I wanted the girls to learn updated language, but not now. I jot down a note for myself to teach them about this later.

Before I can ask Jesse a follow-up question, Lydia—a freckle-faced teenager with brown hair braided in pigtails—blurts out, "I just want my parents to tell me the truth about my adoption. They think I can't handle it, but I can! I just want to know why I had to be adopted."

In typical Adoptee Lounge fashion, we explore these topics, inter-weaving them with silly teenage antics and stories about the latest fad on Instagram and Tik Tok challenges. After the session concludes and I am straightening up the classroom, I notice Lydia hasn't left. She begins helping me stack the chairs and says, "My mom calls my birth mom my 'tummy mommy' and says that I grew 'in her heart.' But I know that I grew in my birth mother's uterus—not her tummy. And, unfortunately, I had to find this out the hard way."

I ask her what she means, worried she will be late for her next class, but also wanting to be present with her in what feels like an important moment.

"I know that babies grow in a woman's uterus," she declared. "But, yesterday I told my whole class that I grew in my mom's heart. And I meant it, even though I knew it couldn't be true." She said the whole class laughed at her.

For years, Lydia's mom used the "you grew in my heart" metaphor to make clear that growing there is better than being born to someone who couldn't keep you. She surely meant no harm by this. But metaphors are powerful. They offer concrete visual images of hard-to-understand ideas. Metaphors can go beyond just helping us comprehend ideas; they can change the way we unconsciously think of a concept. For example, in 2011, sociologists Paul Thibodeau and Lera Boroditsky conducted a study about citizen response to a crime wave.[1] Half of the participants read about the uptick in crime as an animal metaphor: a beast preyed upon innocent citizens. The other group read essentially the same de-scription of the city but were given a medical metaphor: a disease plagued the town. When the subjects were asked how to solve the crime issue, those who read the animal metaphor suggested control strategies like increasing police presence and imposing stricter penalties. Those who read the medical metaphor suggested diagnostic or treatment strategies, such as seeking out the primary cause of the crime wave or bolstering the economy. The study showed that the wording of the metaphor changed the way readers thought about the crime issue. If it was a beast, it needed to be controlled. If it was a disease, it needed to be treated. Metaphors subconsciously control our perceptions.

"I feel incomplete," Lydia says, twirling one of her braids around an index finger. "When my mom says that I grew in her heart, it makes me feel like an alien. I know she loves me, but someone else gave birth to me and I wish she'd admit that and let me know who that person is."

Lydia reminded me of Ashton and the framed quote that her parents hung on her wall. Both girls were experiencing a clash between cultural narratives and personal truths. It was bound to happen as cultural narratives aren't often about the truth. For Lydia and Ashton, it was becoming difficult to assimilate into their adoptive families without understanding the full unvarnished details. Many adoptees are told that their lives are better because of adoption. Appreciating the love, security, and stability our adoptive parents provide could all be undone by our striving to know the story behind the adoption. The tensions in the Adoptee Lounges are due to the feeling that yearning for answers about our birth family or adoption makes us seem ungrateful.

For Lydia, the heart-growing metaphor confused and stifled her. It turned her quest to find language for what she'd experienced into a tightrope walk that she only felt comfortable exploring in the Adoptee Lounge. The way her adoptive mother's emotions are wrapped up in the metaphor made it exceedingly difficult for Lydia to label her adoption as the trauma that it is. The risk of undermining her parents' emotions was simply too great—so great that it led her to forego what she knew about anatomy to fit her emotional desire. That desire to believe her mom's words. That desire to be claimed. *You grew in my heart.* For Lydia there was only room for one set of "real" parents.

I am grateful that for as long as I can remember, both of my parents demonstrated that they were able to hold two conflicting emotions at the same time. They fearlessly understood and named the paradox that they were so happy I'd joined their family and also longed for a world in which Deborah could have kept me. They never balked or seemed scared when I asked questions about my birth family or why I was adopted. Perhaps they felt more than they showed. But to me, it seemed they understood that my ability to hold multiple truths at once would be bolstered by their modeling of this. Because of this, I was allowed to claim my adoptive parents, my foster parents, and my birth parents.

Many people shun the idea of becoming a foster parent out of fear that they'll get too attached to the foster child, only to have to let them go. My foster parents, Alison and John, were not those people. They loved me deeply during my first year of life. Because of the unexplained tightness in my limbs, Alison spent hours gently moving my legs in a circular motion in an attempt to loosen them enough to put on or take off my diaper. I arrived to them with the name Angela, which was assigned to me by a social worker. Feeling that to be too detached a method for naming a child, they renamed me Jocelyn-Kate. They recounted their upset upon learning that the name Jocelyn-Kate didn't get communicated to my new parents.

"We were devastated that we weren't able to adopt you," they told me once, explaining that they were uninsured and, given all of my medical needs, couldn't risk putting me in that precarious position. I was eleven months old when my parents came to pick me up, and Alison sent along a T-shirt of hers so I could have one familiar item. I slept with her T-shirt for years. This is how her scent became permanently etched in my senses.

Still, like Lydia, I felt incomplete. When the relinquishment trauma happens before the age of three, the memories of the trauma are stored in the unconscious part of the brain as implicit memories. Implicit memories are not coded in the brain as coherent, but as broken sensory and emotional fragments—images, sounds, and physical sensations. I felt this fragmented sensation as a hole in my heart. Something—someone—was always missing. The traumatized brain responds with fight, flight, freeze, or fawning (people pleasing) when the implicit traumatic memories are triggered.

Like Lydia, I needed more than the vague outlines of my story as presented in the Child Study and the limited information allowed through the closed adoption.

· · · · · · · · ·

In my late teens, I called the state of Tennessee's Office of Vital Records to ask for my adoption records. I was told that by law, I could not make this request until I was twenty-one years old. I turned twenty-one during my junior year of college. This time I was supported by my boyfriend, Bryan, who lived one floor above me in the on-campus apartment complex.

Bryan is long and lanky, but strong enough to give me a good challenge on the basketball court. He and I played at the campus gym any spare moment we had. He fit the profile of so many of the other men at the private Christian university we both attended—white, middle-class, well-mannered, and modest. He had a wry sense of humor and was working toward obtaining a degree in history. He drove around campus in his prized possession, a gold 1967 Pontiac GTO. Just a year before we began dating, Bryan had taken the year off to grieve his father's death. His dad was his best friend, a larger-than-life presence, both in personality and in his physical body. His obesity was due in part to his failing kidneys that were remedied by long car rides for his biweekly dialysis treatments in San Francisco. The hours in the car and at the hospital passed quickly as Bryan and his dad sang oldies and his dad told stories about attending Balboa High School in San Francisco during the race riots of the 1960s. His death was (and still is) a source of great pain, but unlike many of the students at the university, he didn't sugarcoat it with platitudes about how "everything happens for a reason." Bryan also had a sliver of an understanding of nontraditional families because his parents had informally fostered children when he was growing up. Whether it was racism, transracial adoption, poverty, or injustice, I found Bryan to be open-minded, compassionate, thoughtful and—above all—willing to learn. Our relationship flowered during the wee hours of the morning when he was there offering a listening ear; however, others questioned the authenticity of my Blackness in dating a white man. My peers quizzed me on my definition of Black Love, asking whether my feelings for Bryan were a byproduct of being transracially adopted and suggesting a struggle of internalized racism. Tendai Lewis, a Black woman, blogged about a phenomenon called "colonized desires." She wrote,

> White men don't just represent a section of the general public that catch my eye, but a sort of social mobility. Sexual and romantic acceptance become a vehicle of self-validation. In the arms of a white man, I think that some of the issues that I still have and have had with my blackness are resolved in a way. In that moment I'm still black, but more than just black. I'm that special star. I meet some standard of beauty. I'm not too

dark, wide nosed or nappy headed. I'm not loud, rude, or too much. That's the real power that lies in the white male gaze, and that almost transformative power is what I desire. It's not that I don't find other races attractive, but other races can't offer that.[2]

I understood Lewis's premise and the idea of internalized racism; however, I never viewed my relationship with Bryan as a stepping-stone toward societal acceptance. Adoption increased my proximity to whiteness, which impacted my level of comfort with white people. My relationship with Bryan flourished because we fit well together. We understood each other. We supported each other.

Bryan sat with me, holding a notepad and a pen ready to take notes, when I phoned Tennessee's office again. "In order to apply for your records, you need to fill out a form containing demographic information and send a check for $150, plus an additional cost of twenty-five cents per page for any additional pages that might be in your file," the woman on the other end told me.

"How many additional pages are we talking about? Five? Five hundred?" I asked as I beckoned Bryan to grab a calculator.

"I can't know that until I get your file," she said snippily. "And, like I said, to apply for us to get a court order to access your file, you'll need to fill out the form and send a check for $150, plus the twenty-five cents per page."

I understood what she'd said but was trying to figure out the total dollar amount, since my part-time job as a hostess at Dimitriou's Jazz Alley in downtown Seattle covered only enough for my textbooks and rent. I called my parents and asked to borrow $150, letting them know that I would pick up extra shifts at work to pay them back within the month. They obliged. I mailed the application and the check a week later.

Fifty-two days later, I retrieved an envelope in my mailbox with the Tennessee Office of Vital Records stamped in the top right corner. I grabbed a broom and thumped the handle up against the ceiling, signaling to Bryan to come down to my apartment. The broom taps usually meant there was a spider in my room that rendered me useless until it was killed or transported outside. Knowing the severity of my irrational arachnophobia, he always arrived in lightning speed. This time, of course, there was no spider. Instead, I held up the envelope embossed with the state of

Tennessee seal for him to see and ripped it open. Underneath the cover page, I found my birth certificate. The document I'd so long desired.

NAME: Angela E'lise Burt

BIRTHDATE: September 18, 1985

PLACE OF BIRTH: Hamilton County

MOTHER: Teresa Burt

FATHER: David Burt

I was devastated. This document was no different from the amended birth certificate that was mailed to my parents in the months after my adoption. I'd seen that version many times and it was not my intention to get another copy of it. Instead, I was seeking my original birth certificate, which would have listed my birth mother's name, possibly my birth father's, and whatever name was given me in the hospital—maybe just "baby girl." But this amended version had been altered at my adoption to include only my adoptive parents' names. My biological parents' names were not listed anywhere. And there was no need to send additional money because there were no other papers in the envelope. I had been slighted once again. No tears fell, but my simmering anger began to boil.

Amending adoptees' birth certificates is a practice meant to make it seem as though the child was born to their adoptive parents. Amending birth certificates was first proposed in 1931. In the decades leading up to World War II, court records and original birth certificates were sealed to the public to protect the adoptive family from exposure to embarrassment or even blackmail regarding the illegitimate origins of the adoptee. Some amended birth certificates change the place of birth to the adoptive parent's residence. It's a way of legalizing a fiction of "virtue" for unwed women and hiding the shame and secrecy of unwed motherhood. In the 1930s, federal and state laws began appearing that would seal away original birth certificates in order to protect the privacy and anonymity of birth parents who are placing children for adoption. They were also concerned that birth parents and their families could suffer from unwanted contact from adult children whom they placed for adoption. For birth mothers who became pregnant as a result of rape or incest, contact could be a triggering event. Some women hadn't told their family members about the birth and didn't want them to know about their history. For some the amended birth certificates provided protection from unwanted contact that could lead to financial demands. Keeping the original birth certificates locked up and creating new birth certificates with adoptive parents' names helped solve all these potential problems. And in the following decades, the only way to get the original birth certificate released was by court order, which judges rarely allow. This practice continues today.

The state of Tennessee's Office of Vital Records has locked away my original birth certificate. That birth certificate likely lists my name as "Baby Girl" since I didn't have a name until after I'd left the hospital. It would also list my mother's legal name. The father section either states my birth father's name or was left blank if my birth mother didn't know his name or didn't want to share. I still don't know because, to this day, I still have never seen my original birth certificate.

While working at the adoption agency, I saw many other adoptees' original birth certificates and wondered why I, an arbitrary caseworker, got to hold, handle, file, and seal away a precious and personal document, a document that is considered a vital record—one to be stored next to your marriage license and social security cards in a locked, fireproof box. Since the amended birth certificates do not indicate that alterations have been made, many adoptees grow up never knowing that they have an original birth certificate, too. I always hated putting the original birth certificate into a file and locking it away in a vault to gather dust. There were times when filing for the amended birth certificate of a newly adopted child was too emotional for me. It felt treasonous, like a betrayal to myself and to all the other adoptees I knew. I would stare at that piece of paper and feel like I was committing a crime knowing that one day, somewhere an adoptee would desperately want this information and likely never be allowed to view it.

That evening, Bryan and I devised a new plan to crack the code of my life mystery. If my original birth certificate wasn't the path forward, we'd dig deeper and use whatever else was out there to track down my birth family. We found several places on the Child Study where they had forgotten to white out Deborah's last name. There it was, clear as day: Johnson. Google found fourteen million results for "Deborah Johnson

Tennessee" in 0.22 seconds. Facebook had over five hundred accounts for Deborah Johnson. With a common last name like that, we weren't much closer than where we were before.

However, my search happened to coincide with a veritable technological revolution for adoptees searching for their birth families. The ease of searching can create strife for adoptive parents because adoptees can find and connect with their birth parents without their adoptive parents' consent. I remember hearing from an adoptive dad who wrote, "My 15-year-old son Dakota found his birth parents on Facebook." His email detailed the apprehension he had felt. He worried that Dakota's birth mother would be caught off guard seeing that her child had transitioned from female to male. "She named him Danielle. I worry that she won't be accepting of who he is today," he said. Helen Oakwater, author of *Bubble Wrapped Children: How Social Networking Is Transforming the Face of 21st Century Adoption*, says that one of the main reasons adopted youth use social media to search for their biological parents is because the adults in their life have told them a diluted version of their adoption story. "For too many years we have tried to protect children by keeping difficult information from them, but in a digital age this sets them up to unsafeguarded reconnection with the very people who hurt them," she says. The antidote, she suggests, is "100% truth-telling in an age-appropriate way, facilitated by an expert in childhood trauma."[3]

I began my search for my birth mother by joining adoption reunion registries online, which sought to connect birth families with adoptees. I wrote a short paragraph to this mystery woman, hoping that she'd log on at precisely the same moment and write me an immediate response back.

> Hello, my name is Angela. I was born on September 18, 1985, in Chattanooga, Tennessee and am looking for my biological mother and am wondering if that may be you? I found your address online in conjunction with my birth mother's name: Deborah Johnson. If this is you, please know that I am not looking to disrupt your life or pass judgement or blame. I've longed to know where I came from and who I resemble and would simply like to set up a time to meet with you. I've enclosed a photo of myself and my boyfriend, Bryan. Please call me or email me if you get this letter.

I'd sent this letter to ten homes via certified mail, so I could know when and if the letter was received. In the weeks following, four letters were returned as undeliverable. Three people called to tell me that they'd received my letter but weren't my birth mother. I carefully tracked who I'd heard back from and who I hadn't and realized that there was one address that was delivered but no one reached back to me. I inquired about "Search Angels" and confidential intermediaries—people certified by state governments to search adoption files for "non-identifying" information or authorized to contact birth families on behalf of an adoptee, thus protecting the privacy of birth families if they so desire. I began these efforts somewhat naive in my overwhelming hopes. I dreamt that these people could wave their magic wand over the country and that one little particle of fairy dust would land on my birth mother's head, prompting her to call me and tell me who she was and why she so drastically altered my life without leaving any clues.

We called all the Deborah Johnsons in Tennessee we could find through online search queries.

"Hi," Bryan would say to a stranger on the other end. "I know this call may seem random, but my girlfriend is looking for her birth mother. Her name is Deborah Johnson. That's your name, right? Did you have a child in 1985 that you placed for adoption?"

Many people just hung up; others wished us well on our search saying, "I wish I was her!" or "I wish I could help you!" We called nearly two hundred numbers over the course of two weeks but did not find her.

The Child Study provided the first names of my biological siblings, so we began to pair those names with Deborah's last name and sleuthed on the internet for them. We felt like investigators, gaining adrenaline with each click, hoping to find a major piece of the puzzle, but it also felt like a twenty-six-year-long game of hide-and-seek. My biological mother had been hiding from me and maybe she didn't want to be found. I started my blog, hoping that a member of my biological family would stumble upon it and reach out to me.

As time went by, my dearest friends began expressing concern that my search was becoming obsessive. They began to scoff at me, asking, "Why do you need to keep searching? Your parents are awesome, and they've given you everything!" These comments were hard to hear and harder to respond to. Exulansis in a major way. I tried and tried but never quite found the right way to explain my need to find my birth family in a way they could understand. But Bryan's support never wavered. He did not view my obsession as a mere curiosity or a referendum on my adoptive family. He knew finding my roots was a matter of my psychological health and well-being.

One night, while parsing through the Child Study for the hundredth time, he came across a sentence that we'd somehow overlooked. The agency had listed the first name of the man Deborah named to be my biological father.

CHILD STUDY—Part III: *Legal Release of the Child*

On October 16, 1985, Deborah [REDACTED] appeared before the Honorable Judge Payne at the Hamilton County Circuit Court in Chattanooga, Tennessee. Deborah signed a surrender of her parental rights. This agency also submitted for the termination of the parental rights of the alleged father named by Deborah [REDACTED] as Oterious [REDACTED].

How had I missed this? I had read my Child Study hundreds of times at this point, but the name Oterious somehow escaped my vision each time. Had I been so laser focused on finding Deborah and understanding her actions that I overlooked seeing my birth father's name listed?

Googling "Oterious Tennessee" instantly narrowed the scope by about 14 million results. There was one man with that name who lived in Chattanooga, Tennessee. It wasn't long before we found his last name, too: *Bell.* Could Oterious Bell be my birth father's name? We cross-checked by holding the Child Study up to the light hoping that we'd be able to make out some of the letters that had been whited out. We weren't able to decipher the letters, but we could clearly see that there were four spaces whited out after his first name. It had to be Bell.

Bryan searched for *Oterious Bell* on Spokeo, Myspace, Classmates .com, and MyLife while I checked the International Soundex Reunion Registry, which is a site specifically designed for people who have been separated from each other by adoption, divorce, foster care, institutional care, or abandonment. People leave posts up with their information hoping the person they're searching for will happen upon it someday.

I wrote my post on those sites with hope. However, I knew that, even if Deborah had told my birth father that she was pregnant with his child, it is unlikely that he would have known about the reunion sites or any of the other resources for birth fathers. Hardly anyone knows that resources like putative father registries exist. This is a state-run organization that allows men the right to be notified when an adoption of their offspring occurs. But these registries aren't advertised on billboards, park benches, subway cars, or in the men's bathrooms at bars and restaurants. In Ohio, where 56,278 babies were born to unmarried women, only 164 men registered to their putative father registry. In Florida, only 544 men registered while 82,746 unmarried women gave birth. In Virginia, where 35,491 babies were born outside of marriage, 111 men registered.[4]

The poorly designed system reminds me of Justice Antonin Scalia's book *A Matter of Interpretation* and his description of the way Nero, the tyrannical Roman emperor, would post laws high on pillars so they could not be read, and thus offenders could be punished when they invariably broke them.

I knew it was likely that my birth father was one of the millions of men whose parental rights are terminated without them even knowing they had any rights in the first place. Each state has statutes regarding how the termination must take place, but if a woman doesn't name the birth father or the birth father cannot be easily found, his rights can be terminated by publishing a "notice of termination of parental rights" in the local newspaper or mailing a copy of the court termination paperwork to the last known address of the man. The summons in the newspaper often includes details about the approximate date and location of conception. But these efforts rarely result in fathers responding. The laws, you might say, are posted too high up to be read.

"I found him!" Bryan exclaimed, pointing to what he'd found online. A local radio station had posted on its website a blog titled *Sandy "The Flower Man" (Oterious Bell) Could Use a Little Help*. The radio station was raising money to cover Sandy's medical costs.

Sandy the Flower Man was Oterious Bell. Sandy the Flower Man was my biological dad.

My Ghost Kingdom briefly lit up in my imagination, shifting from a proper, almost preacher-esque man to someone goofier, grinning and possibly surrounded by flowers! Real life information pushed my thoughts aside. The blog post was followed by a photo of Sandy the Flower Man.

My mind boggled as I gazed at this man who had my same large, toothy smile, bright brown eyes, and a light brown skin tone. It was a fascinating experience to see a mirror for my looks, personality traits, and interests, triggering a paradoxical sense of connection and disconnection. Bryan and I sat in disbelief, transfixed, staring at the screen. We plugged the moniker "Sandy the Flower Man" into Facebook, and scrolled through picture after picture, analyzing and critiquing every arch and gesture. I went to the bathroom to wash my makeup off to get a more accurate representation.

"It's him," Bryan said definitively, looking at the computer screen and then back at me. "There is no doubt."

I had to go meet him. Then I'd be whole.

PART II

· · · · · · · · · · · · ·

EXPERIENCING

CHAPTER 6

WHITE PRIVILEGE BY OSMOSIS

S EATTLE-TACOMA AIRPORT WAS already bustling when we arrived at 5 a.m. The flight to Chattanooga, Tennessee, had one stop in Atlanta, Georgia, which meant we'd be traveling for just shy of seven hours. I gave Bryan the window seat, knowing he likely would use some of the flight to get some shut-eye. My mom sat next to me, in the aisle seat, directly across from my dad. As we began to taxi down the runway, my mom reminisced about the first time she'd made this trek with me. I was thirteen months old and sat on her lap in the middle section of the airplane. Apparently, I was very social, smiling at everyone around us. My parents loved watching me interact with others, but felt the confused stares, too. They imagined everyone was wondering what this white couple was doing with a Black baby.

"Let's just play out all of the possible scenarios," my mom said to me, as we leveled off at thirty thousand feet. "Would this trip be successful if we met Sandy, but not Deborah? Would you consider the trip worthwhile if Sandy refuses to take a DNA test? What if we don't end up meeting either of them?"

As she spoke, my dad handed her a pack of Sour Patch Kids to give to me, offering my all-time favorite candy to help me process these hard questions. Providing food is my dad's primary way to show love. Each summer the annual "Meatfest" commences in our backyard, where my dad sources the highest-quality steaks and marinates ribs in his own concoction of garlic, soy sauce, lemon juice, olive oil, butter, and parsley picked straight from his garden. While the ribs are marinating, he wraps dates in bacon, then adds the leftover bacon fat to the carnitas simmering in a slow cooker. He places filets of salmon on the smoker and preps the outdoor wood-fire oven for the homemade pizzas that are also on the menu. Throughout our trip, my dad nourished my body and soul with unhealthy, but necessary snacks, a surefire expression of his understanding of the magnitude of the moment. I poured the entire bag of Sour Patch Kids in my mouth and thought about my mom's question.

"I'd like to go see the hospital I was born in," I said. "I'd just like to be on the grounds." I had known many adoptees who traveled to their birth country and felt a sense of belonging. I knew an Ethiopian adoptee who struggled with irritable bowel syndrome and general gut issues, but when he traveled to Ethiopia for a month-long stay in his birth city, those issues subsided. He learned that his body needed the wheat, soybeans, mutton, and other foods that his ancestors had eaten for generations. He continued that diet after returning to America, and his digestive issues have not returned.

In episode number eight of my podcast, *The Adoptee Next Door*, Kristen Garaffo, a woman in her thirties who was adopted from Paraguay to Washington, DC, spoke about this feeling. She traveled to Costa Rica for a yoga retreat, and even though she wasn't even in her home country of Paraguay, and she wasn't there for any reason related to adoption, she felt that her body knew she was home:

> As soon as I got off the plane, I felt my whole body vibrating. I got teary-eyed, and it was sensory overload. My body seemed to remember the heat, the sounds of the birds, the Spanish language that was being spoken around me. And I didn't know why I was so emotional. I didn't figure out that it was my body remembering this place until the end of my two-week trip.

Kristen was caught completely off guard because having been adopted at just five months old, she hadn't ever given credence to the fact that she had experiences prior to being adopted into a loving family in the United States.

As I fumbled around trying to answer my mom's question, I found myself articulating what had been evident, but unspoken. I didn't often think about my birth father. On occasion, I'd catch myself wondering what he looked like and if he knew about me. But I did not ruminate any more than that. Although I was thrilled to have this opportunity to meet him, it wasn't my main objective for this trip. Sandy didn't have a firm hold on my psyche the way Deborah always had. Maybe it's because there was no detail about him or his extended family in the Child Study? Or was my need for connection with Deborah stronger since I'd spent nine months inside of her?

"Honestly," I said, "I just want to look into Deborah's eyes and feel that power of the genetic pull. I don't know what that feels like, but that's what I want." I painted a fairy tale–like story that my mom listened to quietly, nodding and affirming that it made sense this was so important to me. She then gently reminded me that, ultimately, we had no control over how the trip might go and couldn't guarantee the outcome.

As her words sunk in, I switched from speaking aloud to journaling. I wrote the word "hiraeth" over and over in my journal. In Welsh, this word is defined as a blend of homesickness, nostalgia, and longing, a pull on the heart that conveys a distinct feeling of missing something irretrievably lost. Reuniting with biological family members is a world of shifting sand and unclear rules—a minefield of potential disasters. But, for me, as it is for so many other adoptees, the pull to embark on this perilous journey toward mending a disrupted family lineage was stronger than any fear. My journal from that flight was filled with a slew of what-ifs and other unanswerable questions.

"Maybe she'll tell me that she's thought of me every day since the last time she saw me?" I said with childlike hope, popping up from my journal and jostling Bryan out of his nap and my mom from her book. I explained how I felt that meeting my birth mother falls into a rite-of-passage moment. Like the day you get your driver's license, graduate from high school, marry, or celebrate a Bar Mitzvah or quinceañera. I continued along, Bryan and my mom listening sleepily and kindly, respectively, as I wove so much importance into my fantasy scenario.

Eventually, I ran out of words to say out loud. I turned back to my journal but struggled to figure out how to name one of my most persistent fears, even in the safety and solitude of my journal. I feared that Deborah would view me as a racial fraud.

·　·　·　·　·　·　·　·　·　·

Each summer, I attended Camp Lutherwood, which was a haven for me. Located just about a half hour away from Bellingham, about twenty transracial adoptive families from western Washington converged on the campgrounds of a Lutheran church for a weeklong camp that was organized by two adoptive moms and partially funded by the Dave Thomas Foundation. For many of the friends that I made at camp, this was the only week out of the entire year that they got to spend with other adoptees, and for me, it was a time when I felt freedom to explore and bask in being in close proximity to other Black people. At Lutherwood, the people of color outnumbered the white people. The feeling of being in the majority was an unusual, exciting, and empowering experience. In *The Gifts of Imperfection*, Brené Brown describes the difference between fitting in and belonging. She writes, "Fitting in is about assessing a situation and becoming who you need to be to be accepted. Belonging, on the other hand, doesn't require us to change who we are; it requires us to be who we are."[1] At Lutherwood, being surrounded by so many other Black adoptees allowed me to have that intoxicating experience of belonging.

I remember wrapping cardboard tubes in Ankara prints, sealing the end with rubber, then filling it up with rice to create rain sticks. This was where I learned about wax prints, the commonly used material for West African clothing. I learned that the wax print patterns were not random. The patterns represented social standing; certain patterns were worn for funerals and others worn at weddings. There was much more to it than just bold and vibrant colored cloth.

Some nights we'd eat Chinese cuisine, the next night we'd try Ethiopian food. My mom and a few other parents who organized the camp would bring in Black hairstylists to braid our hair. This was where I learned about the ingenuity of Black slaves who hid rice in their cornrows so they had food to plant and grow once they made it to freedom. In South America, cornrows were designed as intricate, hiding-in-plain-sight maps to guide escaping African slaves to freedom. Some refer to these stories as folklore or legend, but the true lesson was in the value of the oral storytelling tradition in Black culture. The practice of braiding hair is an ancient and culturally universal practice dating back at least to 3000 BC. Hairstyles conveyed messages about standards of beauty, identity, and socioeconomic status. In college I learned that my approach was a W.E.I.R.D. way of thinking. I'd been raised in a Western, Educated, Industrialized, Rich, and Democratic (W.E.I.R.D.) manner. Which meant, I was taught to reject history that didn't come backed up with written evidence. In my world, there wasn't room for creative renditions of the truth; nor was their room for the fact that Black people wouldn't be allowed any methods to write out their history—thus the resilience and power of the indomitable Black culture.

One year a Black man who had been on *The Oprah Winfrey Show* came to speak to us. I was excited because it was my first substantive interaction with a Black adult male. I'd never had a Black teacher or Black doctor or known any other Black adult who commanded respect the way he did. The adoptive parents were excited by him primarily because of one of his mantras: "Parents should treat race and racism like sex: you can't avoid talking about it and hope kids end up with the right answers."

Lutherwood was a retreat from the familial chaos and a rare opportunity for social integration with other Black adoptees. My self-esteem blossomed due in part to the racial mirroring I experienced there and the fantastic stories of the resilience of my ancestors. Nearly two decades after my last summer camp experience, I was invited to speak specifically at a larger and hipper version of Camp Lutherwood in Denver, Colorado. The African-Caribbean Heritage Camp took place on the grounds of Regis University, a Jesuit, Catholic university that allowed this camp to use their campus for the week. I arrived to find 150 transracial adoptive families gathering their welcome packets of daily itineraries and information about daily excursion options: zip lining, swimming, basketball, spa massages, appointments for the on-site Black hair salon, ropes courses, and seminars and workshops from keynote speakers and other presenters. I arrived in time to catch the end of one of the speeches and a couple of the follow-up questions. "Given all that I've shared today, how can you expect your Black child to develop a positive sense of self while under your roof and living in a predominantly white community?" the presenter asked. Looking around the auditorium I saw white parents furiously scribbling on their notepads, some wiping tears from their eyes. The speaker ended his speech and asked the audience if they had any questions.

"My husband and I adopted a child from Haiti, and we live in Vail, Colorado," a tall woman with brunette wavy hair began. "It's a beautiful place to live, and our neighborhood loves seeing our Black Lives Matter sign in our yard, but our son is the only Black person in his school. He has never had a Black friend. I understand that you're suggesting we consider moving to a more diverse city, but my husband and I both have great jobs, and we love our home. Is there anything else we could consider doing instead of moving?"

"No." The speaker paused for dramatic effect, looking pointedly at the audience full of white faces. "There is no substitute for Black community. If you want your child to be healthy, you'll ensure that they aren't tokenized and can have a shot at belonging. Next question?"

I felt the discomfort settle over the room. That adoptive mom was probably hoping for an answer that provided some compromise. But she didn't get it. I watched as the mom who had asked the question grabbed her husband's hand and squeezed it tight. I think I saw a tear roll down her cheek. I found it refreshing to hear the speaker give a direct and unflinching answer that didn't acquiesce to the unspoken desire to receive a pat on the back for their awareness. It's a strategy I've tried to employ, but I typically end up using the sandwich method: you open your feedback with positive comments, followed by the main message, and then some final positive comments. If I were him, I might've responded by saying, "Thank you for asking that important question" (*positive comments to open*). "I think it's imperative that your child live in a place where he is not liable to become a token because he's the only person of color in his school" (*the meat*). "But, again, I commend you for asking that question, which I'm sure many other people in the crowd also have. I'm glad you've made it a priority to attend this camp; I'm sure that is a testament to your commitment to instill a healthy racial identity for your son" (*lots of compliments*). I've been working to rid myself of my need to use the sandwich method because it waters down my message.

I slipped out of the auditorium to find room 251, where I was scheduled to lead a two-hour workshop with teenage transracially adopted boys to discuss how to handle racial microaggressions.

A woman with shoulder-length, glossy, blond hair and wearing a "Black Lives Matter" T-shirt stood outside the room awaiting my arrival.

"Hi, I'm your classroom host," she said. She explained that her job was to make sure the microphones, projectors, and any other technology I want to use are working properly. As we hooked up my laptop and set up my lapel microphone, she decided to tell me about her life: "I am the adoptive mother of one of the boys who will be in your class today. He is a twelve-year-old who we adopted from Ethiopia when he was two. I wasn't sure how to tell my son about your class because I try not to talk about adoption or race too much with him. I'm worried it'll make him feel uncomfortable. So he doesn't exactly know what your class is about, but I told him he must attend!"

Inwardly, I cringed but worked hard to maintain a neutral expression. I thanked her for introducing herself and tapped on my laptop, hurrying to finish setting up before the teenagers start arriving. She moved toward the door, but turned around at the last second and said, "Oh, and I've deleted like ten Facebook friends since Darren Wilson's indictment. We are really working hard to make sure that our son grows up in an environment that celebrates him and his Blackness." Darren Wilson was the twenty-eight-year-old Ferguson, Missouri, policeman, who shot and killed Michael Brown, an eighteen-year-old Black man, setting off nationwide protests. This mom was trying to show me how woke she was by congratulating herself for deleting racist friends, but she was also admitting that she avoided having adoption-related and race-related conversations in her home. By bringing her child to this event and not telling him about the class she had signed him up for, she was participating in color-evasiveness.

Subini Annamma, a critical race theorist and professor at Stanford, has offered the concept of color-evasiveness as an upgrade from what used to be referred to as being "color-blind."

"When you choose to be 'color-blind' you've made an active choice," Annamma explains. "There's a paradox there, if you say you're not going to see color, you've already acknowledged it."[2]

I get the sense that color-evasiveness would be a good descriptor for many of the adoptive parents at this camp. They will travel for hours to make sure their child can get their hair done at a Black salon, but they wouldn't choose to move to live closer to that salon. They'll plaster posters of Obama, Martin Luther King, or Maya Angelou quotes on the wall in their family room and will put a Black Lives Matter sign in their front yard but haven't made it a priority to create genuinely meaningful relationships with Black people in their lives.

"No matter how color-blind you try to be, it can't be done," Annamma says. "You're simply evading race."

As I set up my laptop, I pushed back the fear that my role at camp was fulfilling a quota for the adoptive parents. I tried to fend off the sense that I was being tokenized by the adoptive parents. I thought back to Lutherwood and the unavoidable fact that we were operating within white culture. All the adoptive parents were white and all of the kids of color were adopted. There was a handful of white adoptees as well, but given the racial makeup of the parents, the implicit message was that we needed to be saved or rescued by white people. My quiet thoughts were that Black parents must not be able to raise their kids.

White parents are inherently better suited to adopt us.

Since my birth parents are Black, I must be better off being raised by white people.

Assimilating to whiteness will lead to a better life.

Thankfully, this feeling waned as soon as the teens began filing into the room. Seeing them helped me refocus my mission. It wasn't to make the adoptive parents feel like they should get a pat on the back because they brought their kids to this camp, it was to help instill a sense of belonging in these youths. Belonging, a crucial and instinctive need for humans, was something I sought to provide for them, even if only for a couple hours before they returned home. I know from my weeks at Lutherwood that those feelings of belonging can give enough strength to face the rest of the year.

"Please say your name, your age, gender pronouns, what state or country you were adopted from, and then share one experience specifically related to being a transracial adoptee," I said to the fifteen teenage boys who sit in the first three rows of the college auditorium.

"I'll start," I said after a minute of uncomfortable silence and shifty eyes.

"I'm Angela, twenty-six years old; my pronouns are she and her. I was adopted from Tennessee, grew up in Washington State. When I was in high school, one of my teammates sidled up to me after basketball practice and said, 'Angela, you act so white! Always listening to country music and playing piano like Beethoven. You're the whitest Black person ever. You're an Oreo.'"

After another minute of pensive silence, a boy spoke up. With an AirPod still in his ear, he said, "I'm Thomas. I'm fourteen years old, my gender pronouns are he and him." He took a breath. "I was adopted from the Congo and about the Oreo thing, yeah, people call me that, too, but I've embraced it. I'm proud to be an Oreo. I think it's kind of cool because it makes me different and unexpected. I mean, everyone assumes that I play basketball, so they're surprised when I tell them I'm actually a theater nerd."

Thomas glanced nervously around to see how his comments landed. He was displaying a look I've come to recognize in transracial adoptees, stemming from a life of forced assimilation. Thomas's positive spin on a racist comment was both endearing and heartbreaking at the same time. His confidence flanked by a trepid insecurity. Across the room, another pubescent voice spoke up.

"My name is Ethan. He and him pronouns. I'm fifteen years old and I'm a sophomore at my high school. I was adopted from Ethiopia. I live in an Amish village in Pennsylvania." Ethan wore a beanie over his light-brown dreadlocks and a baggy red sweatshirt. "I agree with Thomas."

I prompted him to continue speaking. I was proud of him for speaking up, knowing that everyone in the room benefits when one of us works hard to name the unnameable.

"I guess I just mean that I've embraced the fact that people think I act white even though I'm Black. But, when I get mad, I don't get physical like most Black people do. I just hold it in. I know that Black people shove other people when they get mad. That's not me. Ya'll feel me? I might clench my fists a little, but that's it." He looked around the room, sizing up the reactions as he tested out his code-switching abilities by using African American Vernacular English in this room full of Black people. He seemed to be pleased with the result, because he plunged on: "But, I'm actually dreading seeing my mom after this session. I don't want her to ask how it was. I mean, how do I tell her that I don't like it when she calls me her 'sweet little Oreo?'"

While the boys bantered a bit about how to educate their adoptive parents on racism, I was managing my own triggers. I could practically feel the talons of Ethan's mother's grip on him, and it hurt me to see it so clearly. When white people compare our skin tone to cocoa, coffee, caramel, brown sugar, Oreos, and other sweets, it subconsciously makes us question whether people are truly attracted to us as individuals, or to a flat, fetishized stereotype of us. Deeper still, and more disconcerting, there are links to colonialism in this type of vernacular. In short, what is the best way to show dominance? By eating someone—like in the animal kingdom. I can't help but think of the conquest, genocide, cultural erasure, and other atrocities committed under colonialism.

I took a deep breath and got the room back on track.

"Being called an Oreo is not a term of endearment," I asserted, switching confidently into educator mode, where the cadence of my voice sounds like a church pastor, closing in on their message. "Being not white in this country means that we bear battle scars inflicted from unwelcome stares, taunts, violence, and even microaggressions from our own parents." This got their attention. You could hear a pin drop in this room.

"Psychiatrist Chester Pierce would describe what your mom said, Ethan, and what my high school teammate said as 'microaggressions.'" I explained how Pierce developed his theory in 1970 after noticing that whites were replacing obvious and blatant racism with more subtle but equally powerful racialized language and behavior. "Oftentimes the statements are so small and neither the perpetrator nor the target understands they've participated in racism."[3] I eased off the preacher voice and slid into my therapist-like tone. "Ethan, if you could, what would you like to say to your mom?"

The boys shuffled in their seats, avoiding eye contact. Even though I'd facilitated this type of conversation many times before, I'd never pushed a group of boys in this way. Most of the Lounges I'd facilitated had been primarily attended by adopted girls. I'd imagine that there would be ways that a boy's adoptee identity is impacted by societal stereotypes about gender. Professors at the University of Michigan conducted a study that found "adopted girls had far more interest in, involvement in, and conflict around adoption than boys did."[4] I was thrilled to be in the room with this group of boys who clearly were interested in processing their identity.

Ethan didn't hesitate for long. "I want to tell her to go to a city where there are no other white people. I want her to live there for a week and be called some African-sounding name and then come back and tell me how it felt."

All the boys nodded their heads in rapt agreement. "And we shouldn't even tell her how she got to that city," one boy added.

"Let's only tell her that she is going to love it!" another boy said, feeding off the energy and comradery filling up the room. I smiled and let them go at it for a while, each shouted comment bonding these boys further over the mutual experience of being raised by people who have never experienced being othered based on race, hair texture, eye shape, butt size, lip size, language, cuisine, or nose width. Their comments encapsulated the complexity and confusion simmering below the surface for many transracial adoptees: *How could I undergo a transatlantic slave-type movement across regions in the name of love?* Jennifer Ann Ho, author of *Racial Ambiguity in Asian American Culture*, wrote that the adoptee is "appropriated, assimilated, made into the image and likeness of her parents and society. He is given a (new) name, language, religion, cosmology, worldview; he is, in a sense, colonized—for his own good, out of love."[5]

Susan Harris O'Connor, a Black, white, and Seminole woman who was adopted by white Jewish parents discovered that transracial adoptees have five dimensions to their racial identity: genetic, imposed, cognitive, visual, and feeling.[6] Ethan and Thomas were talking about the difference between their genetic racial identity, which is the DNA inherited from our ancestors, and their imposed racial identity, which is what others say we are.

O'Connor said, "If you are told so often that 'this is who you are,' you buy into that. But the more you can learn factually about your birth origins, the more you can cognitively push back against inaccurate information."[7] When our parents tell us that we're beautiful just the way we are and that it's what's on the inside that counts, it's not enough to counter all the societal patterns that tell us otherwise. Angels are clothed in white. Wedding dresses are white. White means pure and holy. When the Catholic church can't come to an agreement on a new pope, they release black smoke, a universal symbolism for something bad and negative. Villains always wear dark clothing. Supposedly, Hell is dark.

And some adoptive parents, like Ethan's, unwittingly create an unsafe culture in their home that is a breeding ground for confusion. This is what can lead transracial adoptees to be at war with themselves, or at least to feel that they have their feet in two cultures.

We spent some time role-playing responses to microaggressions, and the boys were really into it, getting kind of silly as they played the part of the microaggressors but also taking their responses seriously. We had only a few minutes left but I decided to open it up in case anyone else wanted to share something.

One boy shared that he was scared about learning to drive. He'd heard about Black parents having "the talk" with their sons to help keep them safe if they are pulled over by police. "I don't have anyone to have 'the talk' with me," he said quietly. "How will I know what to do? My white parents have no idea what it's like to be a Black man."

The resonance in the room was obvious. I decided to let the boys talk this out a bit themselves.

"Everything feels different since I hit five eight," one of the taller boys said. "Old white ladies clutch their purses; I get followed around in stores. If I'm not with my parents, it's a totally different world."

"It's like we have white privilege by osmosis," a boy who had been sitting silently in the back row concludes.

They are right. Being in the vicinity of our parents' whiteness affords us privileges typically only reserved for white people. Cheryl Harris, in her landmark legal article, "Whiteness as Property," discusses the transmission of racial identity as one of the most important cultural aspects bequeathed from one generation to the next. Harris suggests that the economic and social benefits from belonging to mainstream American culture are enormously valuable. She calls them the most important heirlooms that a parent can leave to a child.[8]

Harris's work is intriguing; she does not see whiteness as a privilege, but rather as an asset, in economic terms. It wasn't until I went to college that I consciously realized the peculiarity and economic value of being a recipient of white privilege even though I'm not white. I realized how much I'd benefited from being in their vicinity when I was no longer in their vicinity.

Former NFL player Colin Kaepernick is biracial and was adopted by white parents. He once said, "Growing up with white parents, I moved through life with their audacity of whiteness. I assumed their privilege was mine. I was in for a rude awakening."⁹ College was the site of my "rude awakening." It was time for me to learn how to move throughout the world without the white privilege that my parents inadvertently used to protect me.

There is a well-known story of a Black *New York Times* writer, Brent Staple, who countered the stereotype of African American males as prone to violence, by whistling Vivaldi's Four Seasons or Beatles' tunes as he walked at night through Chicago's Hyde Park neighborhood. He noticed that white people seemed to relax, and some even smiled. Staple diffused the negative stereotype by preemptively expressing himself to be educated, refined, and peaceful.¹⁰

Acting white is one of the unintended consequences of desegregation after the 1954 *Brown v. Board of Education* ruling. Most Americans have seen photos of the Little Rock Nine. The nine students were selected by Daisy Bates, the president of the Arkansas branch of the National Association for the Advancement of Colored People, to integrate Central High School in Little Rock. Bates took on the responsibility of preparing the Little Rock Nine for the violence and intimidation they would face inside and outside the school. In the weeks prior to the start of the new school year, she taught nonviolent tactics, provided each of them with intensive counseling sessions after the students were barred from entering the school the first time, and created a strategy to protect them from the angry mob of over a thousand white protesters who had gathered the second time they attempted to enter the school. Once inside the school, the nine Black students faced hostility (even with the protection of the federal troops ordered by President Eisenhower). Bates had to teach them that *acting white* was essential to survival within the schools.

"Some people describe being Black in America as having to be brave all of the time," I tell the boys as our session came to a close. Even though I've facilitated many workshops like this, I'm still amazed at how quickly transracial adoptees find deep connection with each other and how ready they are to share and talk through hard truths. I see that many of these boys came in today worried that they were making a mountain out of a molehill. Now they feel kinship knowing they aren't alone in their experience. These boys were experiencing what W. E. B. Du Bois meant when he coined the term "double-consciousness." "Since the founding of this nation, being Black in America has been a complex mix," I began, as the boys listened intently. "A mixture of embracing one's culture and heritage, while simultaneously employing code-switching, acting white, letting microaggressions roll off us and many other survival techniques. Looked at from this angle, perhaps being a transracial Black adoptee is the quintessential Black experience in the United States."

· · · · · · · · · ·

As we hurtled through the air toward Chattanooga, I feared that my existence, living life in two worlds, would be too difficult to maintain.

My mom broke my train of thought with one more considerate reminder about having realistic expectations. "Let's remember, your right to know your birth family doesn't automatically mean that you have the right to a relationship," she said, adding a nugget of wise counsel: "relationships are a two-way street."

She reached into her purse and pulled out a letter. "If we get to meet Deborah, I've written a letter that I'd like to give her, if that's okay with you." She handed the letter to me to read.

Dear Deborah and family,

I'm Angela Tucker's mom here in Bellingham, Washington[,] and am very excited to be writing this letter. Have thought about this for a long time. Chattanooga had always seemed so far away as our family talked about it over the years but now even though miles apart it feels right next door. It means a lot to Angela and our entire family to be able to meet you and your family.

I'm guessing that you might be curious how we became Angela's adoptive family? The story follows, but first I want to thank you for sharing Angela with us (even though some of you didn't even know you were). We thank you Deborah for choosing adoption. Not only was Angela's life changed by being adopted, but our lives were changed as well. What a blessing this was! Her cheery personality and her "forever" smile brought much joy to our family. People joked as Angela turned 2 years old that I should just hook her to my side with Velcro as she always followed alongside me wherever I went. We were never far apart. Her sports ability—kickball and PE (in elementary school), basketball, track, cross-country and softball in high school and basketball in college—made us all proud. Music also filled our house—her piano, harmonica, karaoke and singing for no reason or any reason was daily. Angela's hearing loss helped educate all of us about both the struggles of wearing hearing aids and the belief that all of life's opportunities were ahead. She added a lot to our family, to say the least.

Deborah, when Angela was born, our social worker told us that your wish was that she be given opportunities in life to live up to her full potential. We took this to heart, felt guided by your request and thought about it many times as we raised her.

David and I flew to Chattanooga a week before her 1st birthday and spent the weekend getting to know her. We met with a caseworker and were given non-identifying information about your family. We spent a couple hours with Angela to get to know her (she slept the entire time!). Then on Monday, flew with her back to Bellingham.

We continued her physical therapy related to her disability but within three months were told by the physical therapist that she had improved enough that she didn't need it anymore. She shortly began to walk, run, and do all the things expected even though there was still some tightness in her legs and arms. Her hearing loss wasn't identified till she was about 4 years old.

And so, this is how Angela became a resident of Bellingham (about 75 miles north of Seattle) and Washington state. As time goes on, I'm sure Angela will share photos, stories, memories etc. about growing up with all of you. (Ask her about getting her wisdom teeth out while she was on crutches, the competition she had with a friend to see who could wear shorts to school every day during the winter of 5th grade, playing basketball in bare feet in Belize, the ride on the Desperado rollercoaster in Las Vegas, our adventure along Highway 3 in Mexico and of course, our annual "Meatfest" BBQ.) And she'll enjoy hearing from each of you what it was like living in Chattanooga.

She has been a joy to our family. We thank you again for sharing her with us. We look forward to meeting you.

Teresa

The letter was moving. And I wasn't surprised to learn that my mom had written it. She was as eager to form a relationship with Deborah as I was. As I had many times before, I marveled at my mom's capacity to share me and all of my siblings with all of our birth families.

Years later, when I told friends about it, they would get downright jealous. At seventy-five years of age, Todd, a gentle man with gray hair and a soft voice, told me I was the first adopted person he'd ever talked with. "I know you might find it odd that I'm reaching out to you," his email began. "I have long been envious of people like you. I feel like transracial adoptees have an easier time talking about adoption with their parents since it's so obvious." Todd was seventy-five when his adoptive parents died. "I've waited for more than seven decades," repressing my emotions about being adopted because if I brought up adoption to my parents, they might think that they weren't good enough parents to me."

We met at Café Ladro, a popular coffee shop just north of downtown Seattle, where Todd lamented that he wasn't sure if he could demonstrate his love for his adoptive parents while desiring to find and connect with his biological mother. He felt forced to show loyalty to his adoptive parents. He wanted to look for his biological family members but felt the need to wait until his adoptive parents died before embarking on a search. Todd lived a life avoiding any encounter with split loyalties.

It is perhaps the most common refrain I've heard from adult adoptees: "Yes, I want to meet my birth family, but I'll search for them after my adoptive parents pass away." I confirm to Todd that his impulse to protect his adoptive parents' feelings is very common. And I am reminded again how remarkable it is that my parents never centered their own emotions in a way that compelled me to protect them at the expense of learning my story. I am clearly in the minority among adoptees, never once believing my search for my birth family would hurt my adoptive parents.

I'd learn later that my mom actually did fear being replaced by Deborah. At the time, I had no clue she held this fear. Had I known this, I might have felt like Todd. I might have repressed my desire so as not to hurt my mom. Her ability to separate her emotions from me and focus on what was best for me is perhaps the greatest gift she's ever given me.

As we started our descent into Chattanooga, I noticed a pregnant woman one row ahead of us on the other side of the aisle. She was continuously caressing her large belly. I stared as she repeated the circular motion over and over. The image transfixed me and my thoughts raced.

I bet she lovingly lacquers her stomach with cocoa butter every day.

I bet she eats only food that her unborn baby wants.

She probably never exercised before getting pregnant, but now she does, to give her unborn baby the best birth experience in the history of births.

My head spun as I stared at her. Of course, she had no idea I was watching her, but her gentle caress of her pregnant belly, her very existence as a pregnant woman, felt somehow directed at me. I found myself silently pleading with her to stop mocking me by so brazenly demonstrating how much love she intended to shed on the baby once born. It felt like a beacon advertising to the world that this was not the case for me. That to even see my birth mother, I had needed to invest work and research and time and money and then to fly across the country. And I still might not even meet her. Maybe not even catch a glimpse of her. My stomach turned at the thought and I forced myself to look away, grabbing Bryan's hand and leaning over to look out the window as we peered down at the city of Chattanooga. I could make out tiny houses, swimming pools, and parks. I made my brain think of only the scenery and would not allow my eyes to shift back toward the aisle.

My first thought when the wheels hit the tarmac: *I am 2,600 miles closer to my biological family than I've been in twenty-five years.* We walked out of the Chattanooga airport and were hit by the stuffy, muggy air that quickly stifled our excitement and slowed our pace both in tongue and on foot. Though we were only outside for a moment, we quickly began perspiring through our tank tops and shorts. An odd confusion rose up in me. This humid southern air felt terrible in my lungs, and I worried how it would affect my relaxed hair. I longed to escape the moment we set foot outside the airport. And this felt deeply wrong to me.

With a jolt, I realized something: for twenty-five years my unquenchable frustration had led me to believe that merely being on my native soil would usher immediate relief. I had imagined it would feel like home. Instead, I felt out of place, disoriented. In one way, it was wonderful to be surrounded by so many Black people; on the surface that felt good. At the same time, though, my Pacific Northwest accent sounded ridiculous compared to the gentle drawls on all the other Black people's lips. I wasn't fooling anyone that I was local. I didn't know this town and I wasn't even sure I liked it. In short, my first fantasy, that some deep genetic tie to the land or the air would be realized in Chattanooga lay broken at my feet.

We'd decided to poke around Chattanooga as sightseers for a day to get our wits about us and adjust to the time change before beginning our search in earnest. As we ventured through Chattanooga, my family seemed to be enjoying the differences in the Chattanooga lifestyle. I noticed their excitement at tasting grits for the first time, ordering sweet tea instead of an affogato latte. They gabbed with everyone who asked where we were traveling from and struck up conversations with locals to learn about major landmarks like Lookout Mountain, the Tennessee River, and the famous Walnut Street Bridge. They were in the honeymoon phase, when everything different was intoxicating. But I was experiencing complete culture shock mixed with a very bad case of "the shoulds."

I should feel comfortable here!

I should fit in here.

I should already know what grits and fried pickles taste like!

Every time I think I "should" be experiencing something, I'm giving in to both external judgment and predetermined failure. In reality, I don't know what grits taste like and I love the heat but loathe the humidity. In my mind, though, I'm trapped by the judgment that I'm meant to be different than I actually am and the belief that in being who I actually am, I'm failing. I know better than to get stuck here. I have worked so hard to not give in to "the shoulds." But the force of this one is stronger than any I've known before. This place is where I was born. I've longed my whole life for belonging and, if anywhere, I *should* feel a sense of belonging here. But I don't. I don't.

As I crawled into the hotel bed at the end of that first day, I found myself nervous about what was to come next. The next day, we were going to try to find Oterious Sandy "the Flower Man" Bell. How would I feel when

I met this man who looked so much like me? Would it be like coming home? Or standing next to a stranger? My dreams that night were filled with anxiety. Bryan shook me to wake me up because I was babbling loudly and thrashing about. I had a vague recollection of a dream where I lost the same thing over and over again.

CHAPTER 7

SANDY THE FLOWER MAN

I STAYED AWAKE AFTER that nightmare and pulled out my laptop. I reviewed every bit of information we'd gleaned about Sandy since first finding him on the Chattanooga radio station website that was fundraising for his medical costs. I returned to the local radio station blog that asked community members to donate money to help cover Sandy's medical costs for cancer. I dug deep into the comments section.

> Sandy is a legend!
>
> Every time I see Sandy, I instantly start smiling.
>
> Sandy fits my description of an angel . . . he seems human in so many ways, but something about him also just seems different.
>
> I know that there are a lot of theories about Sandy. Not sure if he's an addict or if he has post-traumatic stress disorder or something, but I do know that he has the biggest heart.

Dumbfounded by this outpouring of support, I emailed many of the commenters, sharing my presupposed relationship to Sandy and asking if they knew how I could contact him. I received more responses than I'd expected.

> Hello Angela,
>
> Thank you for your email. I sure hope that Sandy is your birth father! He is an amazing fellow. We call him Sandy the Flower Man. His smile lights up any room and everyone wants to trade him a dollar or two for a flower. You two do look very similar, I thought that even before you mentioned it!

Another message read:

Sandy might be homeless, I'm not sure. I don't think he has a phone or a computer, so unfortunately you won't be able to get a hold of him that way. I usually see Sandy on Friday nights, at a local pub where my co-workers and I go to have a cocktail. He has adorned his bicycle with lights, flags, and ribbons. He rides around downtown panhandling for money, but don't worry, he's not like your typical panhandler. He doesn't just ask for money, but local florists donate their extra or slightly wilted flowers and then he gives them out in exchange for a buck or two. Everyone in Chattanooga loves him.

The messages reminded me of the Uber driver who picked us up from the airport and said, "I know y'all aren't from here, but you look a lot like one of Chattanooga's local legends." And the bellhop at our hotel, who grabbed our suitcases and said to his colleague, "Hey, check her out! Don't she look like the Flower Man?"

In just the short time we'd been in Chattanooga, my resemblance to Sandy the Flower Man had already gotten us a lot of attention. Thankfully, in addition to seeing the resemblance, these folks were also helpful in directing us to where we might find Sandy. Our best bet, it seemed, was to barhop to the places Sandy often sold flowers.

That evening, Bryan and I walked from the hotel to the Hair of the Dog, a pub with a pool table and darts. The bartender asked what we'd like to drink without looking up at us. When he finally did glance at me, he exclaimed, "Whoa! You look just like Sandy the Flower Man! Has anyone ever told you that?"

I couldn't get enough of these comments. I'd longed to hear that I resemble someone for as long as I can remember. I could feel tears welling up in my eyes. I didn't want anyone to see me cry, but I couldn't hold them back entirely. Perhaps something in me that I hadn't fully acknowledged craved a meeting with my biological father more than I thought. Perhaps the repeated assertions from strangers of how alike we looked had loosened up some longing in me. Emotionally, I was still just as deeply connected to Deborah as I'd always been—watching a dad play with his two-year-old in the park didn't put me in a trance like the pregnant woman on the plane had. But I found myself ecstatic in an entirely new way at the idea of looking just like my father, a phrase I never imagined I'd be able to say. And what if we had more than just our appearance in common? What if he was also a sprinter in high school? A piano protégé? A fashionista? What if he also poured Sour Patch Kids down his throat in one fell swoop?

. . . .

Nancee, a fifty-year-old woman with light-pink streaks running through her blond hair was adopted as an infant by white parents. She is the chief information officer at a large Seattle tech firm and wears soft purple lipstick. Nancee initially told me that her adoption and loss of her birth family hadn't negatively impacted her at all. She spoke of resilience and persistence and how great her adoptive family is. At the same time, the more we talked, the more I heard traces of discontent, of questions about belonging. Eventually, she began to share memories from her childhood, which she'd always seen as a safe, stable, and unremarkable upbringing. Her parents were quiet, plain-Jane and -John types. They spoke when they were spoken to. But Nancee was bubbly and gregarious. As we talked, she began to realize that she worked hard to tone herself down in order to assimilate into her adoptive family, but consistently butted up against their familial norms.

During one of our lunch dates, she sat back and said, "Everywhere I have turned, from my first breath on this earth, I've been met with detour signs. It's just what happens."

She gave an example from high school when she tried out for the cheerleading squad six times. She kept trying because she simply didn't feel it was ever okay to give up. She spoke about her relationships and how she routinely stays in unhealthy relationships because she is so committed to making them work. Her words reminded me of something Colin Kaepernick said in his Netflix special: "Since the day I was born, I've never been anybody's first choice."

For years I worked with hundreds of couples hoping to grow their family through adoption. In our initial conversations, they shared their motivation to adopt, which was the same story almost every time: unsuccessful bouts of IVF (in vitro fertilization) followed by the heartbreaking decision to move forward with adoption. The tearful statements were often followed up by an eager admittance that they hoped to be one of the *lucky* couples that gets pregnant right after adopting a child.

It is hard not to recognize that society places a higher value on children born biologically than those who are adopted. And yet, I've heard countless adoptive parents say the opposite when talking about their biological and adopted kids: "They're *all* my own!" they insist emphatically. That's what my parents say, too—and I believe them. I know they love all their adopted children as much as their biological daughter. I know they want what is best for each of us.

However, I also know that in response to my sister (my parents' biological daughter) stating that she wasn't planning to have any biological kids, my dad uttered, "Well, the family line stops here." I think it was a Freudian slip. And it stung. But I know he didn't mean it the way I heard it. I gave him a pass, because his language was usually much more inclusive. For example, when people exclaim to my dad, "Isn't it wonderful your daughter got your beautiful blue eyes?" he would respond, "Yup, they sure are pretty. And Angela got her love of reading from her mom." Most of the time, my parents' desire to make sure we all felt included seemed effortless. I knew I belonged in my adopted family and relished in those nongenetic comparisons. I clung to them. But in his "family line" statement, what I heard him say was: the tropical-water-blue eyes, the high intellect, and the perfectly symmetrical faces will stop.

I've spent my life holding many conflicting truths. And here is one more: I always knew I belonged in my adoptive family, and I've always longed for a genetic sense of belonging. As Nancee reflected more about her childhood and adoption, she thought about seemingly insignificant things. Things she called "silly." She loved apple fritters, Peanut M&M's, and Lay's potato chips. As a child, she begged for those foods and was often bummed when her parents came home with maple bar donuts, regular M&M's, and Fritos. This seemed completely arbitrary in her mind until she met her birth family, who began the relationship with a warning. "We have some peculiar quirks you should probably know about," they said to her with a familiar sarcasm. "Anyone who doesn't solely eat apple fritters is crazy. We don't know why M&M's sells anything other than the peanut kind, and the only types of chips we keep in the home are yellow Lay's potato chips."

Nancee was overcome with emotion. It was the moment she realized she didn't have to work very hard with these people who shared her sarcasm and humor. Her kin.

I've heard countless stories like Nancee's over the years. Adoptees, who have always been ashamed of aspects of themselves that didn't fit in with their adoptive family—like a loud laugh or a macabre sense of humor—might find these very traits reflected in their birth family when they finally meet. It's not uncommon for biological siblings to have shockingly similar life stories about what activities, books, and music they love—even though they live two thousand miles apart and never met until midlife.

As we sat at the bar in Chattanooga, anxiously watching the door in the hopes that my biological father might appear at any moment, I felt nerves unlike any I'd known before; I might be about to experience the ease and comfort of being, for the first time in my life, with my genetic kin.

. . . .

"My name is Angela, and this is my husband, Bryan," I told every barhopper who would talk to me. "I was adopted, and I think Sandy might be my birth father. We just flew in from Seattle, Washington, in the hopes of meeting him and finding out if it's true."

Word traveled quickly in the five-block corridor of downtown Chattanooga. Even though I wasn't sure if Sandy was indeed my biological father, people filed into the Hair of the Dog asking for selfies with me and gushing stories about how Sandy had impacted their lives.

> Your dad is responsible for my marriage! He gave me a flower one day, I in turn gave it to a woman who caught my eye at the bar, and we've been married for ten years now!
>
> You are lucky to be his daughter. He is a real special guy!
>
> I know he does seem to have some inner psychological demons, but that smile can't be beat.
>
> The whole town banded together and raised money to get him a new set of teeth after his had fallen out!
>
> Sandy is so fashionable. He has some awesome blue suede shoes!
>
> I've seen him ride a wheelie on his bicycle for about a mile!

The stories were seemingly endless. I was surprised that all of the people who shared stories were white. Downtown Chattanooga is a diverse place, but it was clear that the white patrons had a special affinity for him. I didn't get the sense that Sandy was a local celebrity, but more like the town mascot. When I think of mascots, I think of Mickey Mouse, the Mr. Clean guy, and Tony the Tiger. They are cartoony objects whose features are purposefully exaggerated to be easily recognizable. They are very marketable, quickly adopted by a group of people to serve as a symbolic figure—typically associated with bringing them good luck. Mascots exist solely for the purpose of making others feel good. It's a one-way street. I began to realize that all the comments and emails centered around how he made *them* feel. I wondered if Sandy, this houseless Black man with a larger-than-life smile fulfilled a trope. I wondered if he and I were more alike than I realized. Perhaps we both were hep to the fact that a key to surviving in our respective environments was to be adored by the white people around us.

In the end, we didn't see Sandy that evening. Some people surmised that the side effects of chemotherapy were to blame. We did learn that Sandy spent some nights sleeping under the Walnut Street Bridge, and some people thought he or his mother might have an apartment at the Mary Walker Towers.

Bryan and I relayed our exciting evening to my family back at the hotel. Of course, we'd go to the Mary Walker Towers in the morning, but we agreed it might be best for me to go in alone, rather than bombard Sandy or his mother with the full crew of white folks.

The next morning, we drove to the ten-story low-income housing complex. I exited the van with my heart and mind on fire with anticipation. The name "Bell" was listed in four different spaces on the call box next to the main door. Four separate apartments.

I pressed one of the buttons. A woman's voice was on the other end.

"Hello! Come on up!" she said, unlocking the main door for me without even asking for my name.

I took a deep breath, opened the door to the lobby and looked for the elevator. There was a group of people playing pool and another crowd of folks sitting at a table. Not a white person in sight. Everyone was dressed in brightly colored matching outfits with large Kentucky Derby–style hats. Sundays around 11 a.m. is church time in Tennessee. Back in Seattle, we keep our eye on strangers peering through peek holes, wary of any unplanned guest. But not here. I was greeted warmly by the people in the lobby and showed to the elevator like an honored guest even though they had no idea who I was or what my business was; southern hospitality was on full display. It felt wonderful experiencing the antidote to the Seattle Freeze, which describes the frosty reputation Seattlelites have toward outsiders.

I was surprised that no one asked me if I was related to Sandy since that was all anyone could focus on the night before. I arrived on the fourth floor and knocked loudly on the door. A cheerful Black woman in a wheelchair opened the door and greeted me.

"Hi sweetheart! This is my cat, Gracie. She just loves having visitors." The woman looked to be in her seventies. I took her cue and bent down to pet her cat, while taking inventory of her and her small apartment. Who was this woman with the same last name as my birth father?

"Do you know Sandy Bell?" I asked, following up quickly with the words I'd been anxious to say for the last two decades, "I think he might be my birth dad."

"Why, yes, I do know Sandy." She had a warm southern drawl. "That's my boy! Well, one of them. I've got seven children." The pounding of my heart impossibly got even stronger at these words. Was I looking at my grandmother? She went on quickly. "But no, my boy Sandy don't have no kids. I wish you was my granddaughter though! You sure be pretty."

I spoke quickly, primarily so she wouldn't ask me to leave. I stared at her face, investigating her every feature. We had a similar bright, light-brown skin tone. Her apartment was small and well loved. Even though she seemed resolute in the fact that Sandy was not my biological father, she invited me to sit down.

"My name is Dorothy, but everyone just calls me G-Mama."

G-Mama told me that Sandy comes to her apartment every morning and gives her a kiss on the cheek and a flower. Then he gives flowers to everyone in the community at night. She referenced his recent cancer diagnosis, saying that he'd not stopped by as regularly because he hasn't been feeling good enough to get out of bed.

The more she talked, the more convinced I was that I knew what G-Mama didn't know. The pieces just fit together too well for it not to be true. The chemo, the physical resemblance, the flowers at the bars. Her son, Sandy Bell, had conceived a child, and that child was me. She was talking to her biological granddaughter, even though she didn't yet believe it. I was no longer able to hear her voice as the only sense that seemed to work was my sight. She was radiant. And hospitable. Traits that I'd been told I also possessed. I was lost in the profundity of the moment. I'd found my family.

We spoke for about ten more minutes before I left her apartment. The elevator ride and trip through the lobby were a blur. I wondered if I should have pushed to make her see the truth. Had I blown my chance to meet Sandy and, subsequently, Deborah, because I was mesmerized by my biological grandmother? My parents and Bryan were sitting on a bench in the grassy courtyard anxious for my report.

"I'm pretty sure I just met my biological grandmother," I said. I told them she thinks Sandy is sterile, but I'm certain she's wrong. I'm sure this is the apartment Sandy comes to every morning to see his mother. "But now what do we do?" I moaned. "I can't just ring her bell again and say, 'Actually, you're wrong,' can I?"

But before anyone could respond with ideas, a distinctive sound rang through the courtyard, a kind of metallic but melodic ringing. I looked over to see a Black man riding a bike adorned with bells, whistles, ribbons, and flags pedaling by.

"Sandy!" His name popped out of my mouth before I knew what was happening. I hadn't consciously intended to call out to him, probably because I wasn't prepared to meet him like this. Maybe it was the high I was on from the ten-minute conversation with G-Mama. But something inside me could not let him ride past, not when we were this close. The cyclist stopped, turned his head to look back at me, and strode over beaming his large smile, completely unfazed that a stranger was screaming out his name. I sneaked a glance at Bryan, who was motioning with his hands for me to walk up to him. He and my parents stayed about ten feet behind us. His black faux-leather cargo pants looked like they had been worn a million times, the bottom of his pant legs covered with grass shavings. He had a black cowboy hat and a fake sheriff's badge pinned on his black faux-leather vest which he wore without a shirt underneath. His veins popped out of his arms and chest like little snakes.

With adrenaline coursing through my body, I held out my hand for a handshake. Before I could gather my thoughts, I spewed out my rehearsed lines, "Hi. I think you may be my birth father."

At first, he didn't respond. From the look on his face, I couldn't tell if he was hurt, or confused, or even if he'd heard me, so I continued blabbering. "Is your real name Oterious? I'm adopted. Did you ever know anyone named Deborah Johnson?" He slowly reached back behind him and grabbed a delicate white flower out of the basket strapped to his bike and presented it to me. I kept speaking. It was nervous energy. "Deborah is my birth mother. She listed someone named Oterious as my birth father and I'm just trying to find him." It all came tumbling out. I needed to take a breath. I resisted continuing my soliloquy. Instead, I took a deep breath and reached out my shaky hand to take the flower he offered, trying not to crush it between my anxious fingers.

"Yes, Oterious is my name," he finally said. "But everyone round here calls me Sandy. I'm Sandy the Flower Man." He spoke slowly and proud. He had that same southern drawl I'd heard in his mother. As he spoke, I couldn't take my eyes off him, examining every last detail. We had the same eyes, the same body type and muscle definition, the same smile. His reaction made it clear that he did not know who I was, but he began quietly muttering Deborah's name. I think he was trying to go back in his mind to remember a time when he knew her. It was clear that he had not spent the past twenty-five years waiting for his long-lost daughter to show up. He definitely didn't even know that I existed.

But after a long silence, I realized he was looking at me as carefully as I was looking at him. Shaking his head and releasing a slight chuckle he finally said, "It's like I'm looking in a mirror."

It was indeed. I didn't need Sandy to remember the details of a relationship with Deborah for me to know unequivocally, in that moment in the Mary Walker Towers courtyard, that this man, Sandy the Flower Man, was my biological father.

I motioned over to my family inviting them to come meet him. Sandy shook hands with everyone and invited us to come back to the Mary Walker Towers that evening. He'd apparently quickly made peace with the idea that I was his biological daughter and was ready to show me off and introduce me to the family. Sandy asked us to come back to G-Mama's apartment that night at 6:30 to meet his brothers and sisters. *My aunts and uncles.*

· · · · · · · · · ·

Back in the hotel room I let out a few yelps of excitement and disbelief. I tried on every dress I'd packed in my suitcase, settling on a short black-and-pink sundress with modest two-inch wedges to wear to G-Mama's. I didn't bring any higher heels than that because I wanted to be able to easily measure my own height against my birth family members. We planned to meet my parents in the hotel lobby at 6:00 p.m., giving us enough time to stop by the store to buy a dessert to bring with us. But when the elevator door opened, my mom stood there without my dad. She let me know that he decided not to come but asked us to call him when we were done so we could meet up and tell him all about it.

This stung. My dad had shaken Sandy's hand a few hours ago when we met him outside of the Mary Walker Towers. Why wouldn't he want to get to know him and meet the rest of my biological family?

Does he also fear being replaced?

Did I fail to communicate how his presence was going to provide that same level of comfort that his attendance at all my basketball games provided?

He flew all this way just to back out at the last second?

It didn't cross my mind at the time that perhaps he just needed more time to process the encounter. That it might have shaken him in an unexpected way to meet Sandy and see the strong resemblance between us. We'd all focused intensely on my birth mother for the past twenty-five years, giving my mom ample time to process and settle into her role as a mother to a daughter who has another mother. My dad hadn't had that opportunity, or perhaps the feminization of the adoption discussions prohibited him from processing this earlier on. In an article titled "About Paternal Voices in Adoption Narratives," author Fu-jen Chen points out the lack of discourse about adoption from the adoptive father's perspective:

There is a stunning volume of maternal voices—mostly by adoptive mothers (as adoption experts or biographers) and birth mothers (as memoir writers). In the last decade, adoptees have become aware of a great demand and urgency to articulate their own unique life experiences. Those who call for an authoritative voice and an identity specific to the adoptee are mostly women. They are looking for their "birth families and those searching are most frequently looking for birth mothers, not birth fathers" . . . and their stories "are almost always stories about motherhood," not fatherhood; about motherland, rather than fatherland. Because the conversation about adoption has been dominated by women (specifically maternal figures), its major concerns are thus oriented towards womanhood, motherhood, and mothering.[1]

The dominance of female perspectives reminded me of a mentorship session I'd had with Naveah, a fourteen-year-old adoptee. Over the two years that I'd mentored her, she'd consistently spoken of and wondered about her birth mother. I asked if she ever thought about her birth father.

"I don't have one," she replied.

I was confused at first, wondering if she was being facetious. But given the straight look on her face, I soon realized that she wasn't. She meant it.

"In order to be alive, we all were created by two people. You do have a birth father," I said, gathering up my courage to have the birds and the bees conversation. She responded with evidence that she knew how babies were made but simply had never thought that she had a birth father. Kristine Freeark writes, "We know that adopted children fantasize and wonder about their birth parents as they get older, but such fantasies focus almost exclusively on images and explanations about their birth mother's behavior and children tend to be virtually amnesic about their birth father."[2] Naveah's world expanded at that moment. She spoke quickly during that next hour as she began to wonder about her birth father's story.

· · · · · · · · ·

The drive to the Mary Walker Towers crawled by. My mom drove the speed limit, but that was too slow. We stopped at a store to purchase something to bring to the party. It took too long. Bryan opened the car door holding a cheesecake and I snapped at him, even though he'd been in the store for less than five minutes. I was beginning to panic and hy-perventilate. My sense of time was completely warped—partly by nerves and excitement and, in a different way, by growing up in white culture. To me, being on time means arriving and parking at the intended location five minutes prior to the start time. To my biological family, I would soon learn, "on time" means thirty minutes after the stated start time. This was one of the first and most obvious cultural differences between myself and my kin. Colored People Time (CPT) is a way to describe habitual and acceptable tardiness. Although it felt unnatural and irresponsible to me then, it turned out we were right on time.

Walking back into G-Mama's apartment, I noticed that she had changed her wig since earlier in the afternoon. She was radiant. Smiling ear to ear and asking repeatedly for me to give her a hug. Her five-hundred-square-foot apartment felt too small for me, my emotions, my three aunts, three uncles, cousins, and in-laws. People kept piling in and with each person, more laughter, more chatter. The decibel level reached a point where I needed to adjust my hearing aids. I stared at Sandy as he introduced me to everyone. I watched how his lips moved when he said certain words. I studied his southern accent and his clothing choice. I examined his head shape and the length of his fingers. He wore a bright blue, silky button-up shirt, black pants, and a fedora. I loved how he and I both chose loud, bright clothing and neither of us could stop smiling.

Sandy's family is not a quiet bunch. Everyone talked at the same time and there was lots of loud raucous laughter. The noise level was high, the energy and fervor in the room was palpable. I loved seeing reflections of me in each of them. I was known by my friends to laugh so hard that I cried. I think nearly all my biological family members were crying from laughter at that moment. It was beautiful and I loved it even when I couldn't understand all that was going on because the volume and overlapping voices made it hard for me to listen to every single word.

Growing up in our house in Bellingham, interruptions weren't toler-ated. A sign of a good time was a quieter function where everyone was given a chance to speak and be heard. This was how we learned to com-municate respect. It also helped me to be able to hear. My hearing aids are helpful, but I also read lips to understand what is being said. To do this, I need to first identify where the sound is coming from, then focus on the speaker's lips and watch while listening closely. I couldn't do that at G-Mama's house that night, but I wasn't yet ready to tell them about my hearing loss—especially since we suspected that it was due to drug use in utero. I made eye contact with Bryan and telepathed, "I can't understand what everyone is saying." Depending on the environment, this signals to Bryan to either whisper in my ear or write a few notes on a piece of paper to summarize what had transpired. That is the strategy he used at that moment. He whispered to me that my uncle Jay was talking about his career as a professional boxer. My aunt Pam was talking over him, excitedly adding to his story by talking about her time as a Ring Girl, where she'd wear a bathing suit and walk around the boxing ring, holding up a large card with the match number on it. "Your uncle was a middleweight boxing champion!" Bryan whispered to me. I finally was able to make sense of the large glittery belt he had brought to show me. "At least now we know where you got your athleticism from!" Bryan quipped aloud to the whole group. "We don't just say he's got that million-dollar smile for nothin'! Those white folks paid some kind of money for this," Uncle Jay responded.

I noticed Uncle Jay and my other uncles used the words "white people" a lot. "Do you white people really eat mayonnaise with everything?" Jay asked Bryan and my mom.

I noticed their lighthearted and fun nature extended to all things, including jokes about racism. "White people be like, 'I'm not just white; I'm 22 percent Irish, 18 percent German, 28 percent Italian, 30 percent French, 2 percent milk,'" someone said, creating uproarious laughter. "Yeah, I bet Taco Bell is too spicy for you, Bryan, huh?" they jeered. Bryan, the only white man in the room, would nod in amusement signaling that he could handle their jokes, so they kept them coming.

For most of my life, I had been the only Black person in the room. Any time white people got uncomfortable or felt offended, I found myself easing off or offering support for their fragility. But in Chattanooga, in this room full of Black people, it was different. For the first time, the jokes weren't at my expense. And it was the first time I didn't feel a need to come to the rescue of a white person. Instead, I got to laugh along with Sandy and Uncle Jay as they teased Bryan about white people's food tastes and stiff gait. I was confident that Bryan knew he was on their turf and to talk back in any way would be centering his whiteness and muzzling all the Black people in the room. I'd heard that comedians have an unspoken rule that you can't make fun of people who have less privilege than you. It's why LGBTQ comedians can make fun of straight people, why single people can make fun of married people, why women can make fun of men. I enjoyed every second of this delightful, new comradery I felt with my kin.

"Sandy, did Deborah ever tell you that she was pregnant?" I cut into the festive, fun atmosphere with a searing question that I simply could not wait any longer to ask. "How did you two know each other?" I knew that would be an uncomfortable question for Sandy to answer in front of his entire family, but I had to know and wasn't sure I'd get another chance to ask it. This energetic party at G-Mama's house felt so easy and joyful but my laser focus on Deborah remained, even while in the presence of my new biological paternal family. I just plopped into Sandy's family out of nowhere. But Deborah has known about me for twenty-five years.

"Well, I do remember talking to her back in the day."

"Talking," sounded to me like they were friends with benefits, somewhere between dating and a one-night stand. Sandy's siblings chimed in, offering vague descriptions of what they remembered about Deborah. Some said she worked at a gas station; others said they thought she drove a school bus. None of their answers were coalescing into a tidy bow.

I pushed on: "From our internet sleuthing, we found several addresses that might be hers. I have sent letters to all of them but haven't heard back. There is one address that seems to be the most recent. I'd really like to meet her, but I don't want to ambush her." I truly didn't want to ambush her, but I also felt that I had to pack a lifetime of longing into this little sliver of opportunity.

"Ah, the Avondale neighborhood. Yeah, I bet Deborah live over there," said Sandy, definitively. My heart caught in my throat. Could it be that easy? I mean, anyone looking at Sandy and me together knew we were genetically related. And without prying too much into the details of his sex life twenty-five years ago, it seemed clear that Sandy was not denying a relationship with a woman who had the same name as my birth mother in the Child Study. I almost couldn't breathe as I realized how close I suddenly was to Deborah.

Sandy's brother Jay jumped in with what I was coming to recognize as his signature boisterous, charming style. "Well, let's get on over there then!" he said, jumping up. "Why waste time? Ain't this beautiful young lady already been waiting her whole life?"

And just like that, it was decided that Uncle Jay and Sandy would drive us through the neighborhood where Sandy thought she lived. I was thrilled at the possibility that I'd get to see her house.

CHAPTER 8

UNCLAIMED

CHILD STUDY—Part II: *Family History*

Deborah is presently residing in a government housing project in the Chattanooga area and is currently being supported on the state welfare system. Deborah hopes to return to school to complete a degree so that she is able to earn a living for herself.

A S MY UNDERSTANDING of poverty and its inextricable link to racism in the United States grew, I found myself wondering whether my adoption allowed Deborah more opportunities. Perhaps on some level I even believed that I could deem my adoption a success if Deborah rose out of poverty as a result.

But as we drove into the neighborhood, it became clear that the people who lived here were below the poverty line. The street was filled with potholes, feral animals ran about the neighborhood, abandoned cars littered the grassy patches, and people sat on dilapidated stoops of brick shotgun-style houses. Shotgun homes got their name because it is said that a shotgun could be fired through the front door and its pellets would emerge from the rear of the house without hitting an interior wall. Looking around, I didn't doubt that happened in this neighborhood. We were a spectacle before we even set foot outside of our large rental suburban with its tinted window.

But with Uncle Jay leading us in his black SUV, we probably looked like some kind of security detail. The car rolled to a stop directly in front of the address that I had written a letter and sent a photo to just five months before. The house looked like the others in the neighborhood, possibly even a bit more unkempt. If this was where my birth mother lived, she most certainly had not risen out of poverty.

I was taking everything in, squinting to try to see through the black garbage bags that were taped to the front window. I wanted to get a glimpse of the woman who lived there but was dealing with plenty of emotions just being this close. Seeing the neighborhood provided me with more information about my birth mother than I'd had in years and left me with plenty to process. I hadn't imagined just being in the neighborhood would make me feel so out of my element, uncomfortable—scared, even. What did that mean? I was ready to drive back to the hotel and talk about a new plan or simply head back to Seattle. Bryan felt my tension and looked like he was about to turn the car around when, to my dismay, Sandy grabbed the door handle and jumped out. Without saying a word to us, he walked straight up to the front door. *This was not the plan.*

Uncle Jay got out of the car and walked over to me. "Don't set her off. Try to keep everything friendly," he mumbled under his breath. Then he followed after his brother.

I sat frozen in the car, unable to move, unable to think. My mom reached over to squeeze my hand which was both comforting and ended my trance. It dawned on me that any second, the moment Sandy knocked on that front door, I could see my birth mother in the flesh. I was not ready for this. My body was tense and frozen.

"She in there!" A neighbor shouted at Sandy from the stoop next door, "She hasn't come out for a few days, but I seen her lights come on from time to time."

The front door opened and a short, round woman stepped out. Realizing that my twenty-five-year-long game of hide and seek was about to end threw my brain into a tailspin. In the weeks leading up to this trip, my therapist had taught me three grounding techniques for moments when I needed to distract myself from difficult emotions. One strategy was to describe my environment in granular detail, using all my senses. For example, I'd say, "My back and thighs are touching the black leather of the bucket seat in the tall SUV. My fingers are wrapped around the cold, shiny, silver door handle . . ." Another strategy was to hold an ice cube in my hand or run very cold water over my hands. The last was to simulate playing Pachelbel's Canon in D on the piano, by tapping my fingers on my legs. This was definitely the moment to begin employing one of these strategies. I began playing my imaginary piano.

I don't remember opening my door and walking across the street to join Sandy and Jay, but somehow, I did. Bryan turned on his camera and began filming. He had vowed to document moments I'd be too overwhelmed to remember. He held his camera discreetly hoping not to attract attention. Sandy and the woman walked toward the middle of the street. The woman wore a purple shirt and black leggings. She was short and overweight, with a scraggly gray Afro.

"Hi, my name is Angela." I said in a syrupy sweet voice that I'd practiced millions of times before. "I think you may be my birth mother." I've never felt my heart pound so fast; each rapid beat crashing against my ribs as though to break through.

"No," she said without skipping a beat in a hard-edged and scratchy voice. With one hand on her hip and the other holding a cigarette, shoulders slumped, and her head bowed down, she said, "I ain't have no children. I'm sorry, but I ain't the person you looking for."

I can't remember if she said the words "get off my property." But if she didn't, it was certainly inferred. I think at that point, I went numb. Perhaps my nervous system was so overloaded it just decided to take a break. I don't remember crossing the street and climbing back in the van. But evidently, I did. As we drove away, I heard myself say, "That is such a bummer that we got the wrong person!" There was a long pause as my family exchanged looks with each other. Finally, my mom spoke.

"No, Angela," my mom said gently. "That was her. You just met your birth mom."

. . . .

I am always smiling and always get comments about my sparkling white teeth. The few teeth that Deborah had were brown. People always talked about my positive and cheery disposition, but she seemed angry and mean (understandably so, given that I'd just shown up at her door). Her body was slumped over, and her head hung low. I stood tall, with my head held high. *That couldn't be her.*

I thought back to sections of my Child Study where they described my birth mom twenty-five years ago.

Deborah is 4' 11".
She is overweight.
She has black hair with streaks of gray.

The woman at the shotgun house fit that description. And she greeted Sandy at the door in a manner that indicated she knew him. They didn't hug like old friends who hadn't seen each other for decades, but clearly, they were acquaintances. She was living at one of the addresses we had found online. I wanted to believe what she said, but the facts said otherwise. And everyone in my family was certain it was her.

It was beginning to dawn on me that I'd just met my biological mother. That was Deborah. That was Deborah? But it couldn't be her! She didn't embrace me. She barely looked at me. It wasn't like looking in a mirror, it was like looking into a deep, murky pond with no reflection at all. No. That can't be the end of all this searching. That can't be the end of my story. That we found her. And she still doesn't want me.

It was a second rejection. The first rejection was when Deborah left me at the hospital alone for the social workers to deal with. But that rejection was different. It was more passive; I wasn't consciously able to understand what was happening. However, seeing her face-to-face as an adult and being turned away was as though I was standing there saying, "I exist!" and her response was "I wish you didn't." It was a turning point in my quest to intellectualize the whole experience because, although my brain wanted to justify this recent encounter as an understandable response from someone with such a deep well of shame, my heart didn't agree. I wanted to give her the benefit of the doubt and offer understanding that my presence may have been too intensely related to past hurts, that my presence was just too frightening and she didn't know how to respond to me; but truthfully, my brain wasn't winning this argument. My heart was and it was shattered.

As we drove back to the hotel, I felt as though I were a butterfly encased in resin. A silence filled the car. Everyone seemed unable to speak, as though the wrong word might pierce some kind of balloon full of painfully intense emotion that would spill into the car, overwhelming us all. Perhaps they were just trying to give me space to process.

I soon found myself back at the hotel, sitting on the edge of the bed. I realized that I needed to pee after I kicked off my shoes. But instead of using the restroom, all I could focus on was the twenty-eight-second video Bryan had taken. The room blurred around me; the only thing in the room was the tiny camera playback window. I watched the video clip on a loop for forty-five minutes. It was like a GIF, except there was no punchline. I was locked in with a laser focus and too far outside my body to attempt any of the grounding techniques. Finally, Bryan decided he had to shake me out of it.

"Angela! You need to stop," Bryan said kindly, with a sturdy yet loving shake of my shoulders.

"We're going to go to dinner in half an hour. Your dad wants to hear about our time with the Bells."

Blinking back tears, I swallowed hard as the room and Bryan came into focus. I felt a tiny bit lightheaded; food will be good. As I stood up and moved toward the shower, my thoughts became more conscious but remained fixated.

Does Deborah's right to privacy trump my right to know my story?

Why is she denying me? Did I do something wrong? Should we have approached her differently?

I survived one rejection from my birth mother, but could I survive a second?

· · · · · · · · ·

While working at the adoption agency, I met Heather, a nineteen-year-old white woman who was eight months pregnant. The only people who knew about her pregnancy were the strangers who were allowing her to live in their trailer in exchange for cleaning their home. They paid her ten dollars an hour. She was saving to pay for an ultrasound, which would cost $250. Some weeks her landlords didn't have any cleaning needs for her, which made it hard to reach her goal. So she wrote her landlords a letter, asking for a $250 loan and describing the nature of her request. They loaned her the money. However when she tried to leave after her ultrasound, the doctors wouldn't let her go without making a connection with the local adoption agency first.

"Hi, Angela, I'm only calling you because the doctors are making me. But I want to make clear, I don't want to give up my baby." She began to break down in tears. "They also told me I'm having a girl and she'll probably be here in a week or two." I learned later that Heather ran away from home, where she had witnessed domestic violence altercations for much of her life. She was homeless and unsure of who the father was. After many discussions about her situation and brainstorming resources that might be able to support her to keep her baby, Heather reluctantly asked me to find a financially stable, married couple to adopt her unborn child.

I scrolled through the list of names of prospective adoptive parents. The people on the list all had completed home studies. The home study is a process where prospective adoptive parents are interviewed by a licensed professional about all aspects of their lives, including finances, mental health, physical health, and marital life, to determine their overall fitness as parents. The result is a document that is submitted to the courts at the time of the adoption.

It was almost a year ago when I visited the Mitchells' home for their final inspection. They had a mansion on the water in Seattle. One bedroom was expertly decorated for the baby they hoped to adopt, but they kept the door closed because it was too painful to be reminded of what they didn't have yet wanted so badly. As part of the interview, I asked them about their adoption preferences. *Did they want a boy or a girl? A newborn, toddler, tween, or teen? A Black child? Latinx? Native? Asian? One who has had previous adoptive or foster placements? A child with developmental disabilities?* In theory, this is supposed to ensure that the child is placed in a home where the adoptive parents can meet all the child's needs, but I worried that I was participating in a process that ushered in a false confidence since I cannot promise an unknown.

"We are only open to adopting a newborn white girl, so long as the birth mother has not done any drugs or smoked while pregnant. We've heard that it can have some lifelong impacts on the baby. We also want to be able to choose the child's name and choose how much contact the birth mother can have with our child as she grows up," Mr. Mitchell said.

On one hand, I'm really glad that they knew their limitations. They knew that they were not equipped to raise a child with disabilities, and they did not have a diverse friend circle or community, so it would not be right to place a child of color into that home. On the other hand, it was a strange experience to conduct a process that allows people to choose characteristics that they want in a child, as if they were swiping through Tinder profiles.

Jill Dziko, an adoptive mother who investigates prospective families and writes their home studies, notes,

> One of the most damaging and least talked about problems is the pressure put on white families to "broaden" their adoption criteria. And by "broaden" most adoption agencies mean racially. White Adoptive families are told they can adopt faster and less expensively if they are open to adopting a child of color. . . . As the cost and wait times to adopt have climbed so has the pressure to approve adoptive families to adopt trans-racially. Over the last couple of years, I have had several agencies attempt to "strong arm" me into changing my homestudy recommendations to approve families to adopt trans-racially when I was firm in my professional assessment [that] they were not prepared to parent a child of a race different than their own.[1]

I was grateful that the Mitchells weren't trying to adjust their preferences, but on the other hand I couldn't help but feel some personal pangs of hurt. *They wouldn't have wanted to adopt someone like me!* It felt like they were judging me without even knowing it. I redirected my hurt by going to education mode, using that preacher-type voice. I reminded them that adopting a newborn cannot happen without a precipitating stressful event for the pregnant woman and that the stress of a pregnant woman may leave lifelong psychological or medical impacts on the baby, just as drugs or smoking may. I wanted to make sure that I wasn't overpromising and underdelivering. Even if they were able to adopt a child within their criteria, there may be unforeseen issues that arise. The simple nature of enduring an unexpected pregnancy can be stressful to a baby. I was attempting to humanize women who face unexpected pregnancies and who may not have financial resources or family support.

Over the course of the next eleven months, they turned down twenty-two opportunities to adopt. None of the unborn children perfectly matched their preferences. Each time they passed on an opportunity I felt the pain of the double-edged sword. I was thankful for their honesty. By saying "no," they were helping to ensure that they didn't end up with a child they didn't feel equipped to raise, but I also felt deeply conflicted about the shopping-like process.

When I presented them with Heather's situation, they were interested.

Heather, the Mitchells, and I met at a Starbucks in Seattle two days later. The Mitchells pulled up in their slate gray Cadillac Escalade. They were dressed in their Sunday best, eager to meet Heather. Heather arrived twenty minutes late after taking three city buses. Her clothes were a bit tattered, and her energy level seemed low. The moment of the initial meeting is always awkward. I try to take the lead to eliminate the need for either party to break the ice.

"Hi, Heather, how was the bus ride?" I said deliberately, before officially introducing her to the Mitchells. I wanted to set the tone for the meeting by centering Heather. Some of the pregnant women I'd worked with had told me that these meetings have made them feel like a surrogate. Mr. Mitchell outstretched his hand before Heather could answer me. He held a beautifully wrapped gift for Heather with a note on the outside:

> We view adoption to be one of the most selfless choices a woman can make. And if you choose us to be the adoptive parents to your child, we will strive to match your level of altruism.

The Mitchells pulled the chair out for Heather as she wobbled to the table and placed her hand on the table for balance. I was conflicted by my facilitator role and the intersection of competing values and basic societal assumptions. Was I helping to "save" a child from Heather's impoverished world, or was I helping the Mitchells realize a dream they felt entitled to create? Heather shared about her current living status and told them that her water could break any day now. The Mitchells listened dutifully, leaning in toward Heather and making sympathetic noises and gestures as Heather cried and spoke about how she wished she could parent this baby girl.

"Heather, if you entrust us to parent your baby, we will love her with all of our heart. We have a name picked out and have already been looking into swim classes for infants. We're already on a wait list at a Montessori preschool just three blocks from our house."

After the meeting, I walked Heather out to the bus stop. As the bus pulled up, Heather told me that she liked them and that it'd be okay if they adopted her baby. As she stepped on the bus, she looked back at me and said, "They can have my baby, but would you ask them if I could hold my baby first?"

CHAPTER 9

FILLING THE VOID

T HE REST OF OUR TIME IN Chattanooga and the plane ride home were a bit of a blur. My mom was researching the meaning of "Pure-D," a word Sandy used often in reference to how he felt about me finding him. "It's a Pure-D miracle!" he'd exclaim repeatedly throughout the day. My dad kept shoveling the snacks my way, and Bryan didn't sleep a wink, watching me carefully. Perhaps they all worried just a little that the pain of Deborah's rejection would erupt at any moment, disrupting the steady, almost numb calm I'd taken on since watching the video in the hotel room. They needn't have worried. I quelled the hurt of being rejected by Deborah in the same way I did anytime life felt too chaotic: music and intellectualization. I obsessed over one song and explained away my emotions through academic research. The combination of these two coping mechanisms, which I'd honed to perfection my entire life, prevented the Deborah-shaped hole in my heart from growing any larger.

When I was thirteen years old, my family piled into our green minivan for a long road trip from Washington State to Cabo San Lucas, Mexico. The trip down the West Coast was full of sibling antics, bathroom stops, McDonald's meals, "I spy with my little eye" games, and for me, there was music. One song, by the Goo Goo Dolls, the post-grunge phenom of the late 1990s, took deep hold of me. The song was called "Acoustic #3" and although it is just one minute and fifty-three seconds long, I listened to it for more than thirty hours over three days of driving.

The soothing straightforward sounds of "Acoustic #3" felt stable and grounding. It wasn't the lyrics that sucked me in, it was the canonical strumming of the guitar on the G chord and the soothing stroke of the bow on the cello. Most songs start in a home key, then depart toward a rising tension, leading to the bridge of the song and ending with a resolution before bringing us back to the home key. But this song didn't do that. There wasn't a bridge. There wasn't any tension. The song never deviates from the home key. The total lack of dissonance soothed me, creating a perfect world, void of the hard realities of my life, a soundtrack perfectly fitting my Ghost Kingdom, two minutes of total ease and complete resonance—so different from what I often experienced outside my headphones.

About a week into our vacation, on the pothole-ridden, tire-busting Highway 3, somewhere between Ensenada and San Felipe, we found ourselves stopped at a makeshift security checkpoint. A dozen teenagers with large machine guns lined us up outside of our minivan. We were all terrified. Even though they spoke Spanish, we understood that they were demanding all of us vacate the car so they could inspect it for drugs. Our Washington license plates, the unusual racial makeup of our family, and my sister's bulky black wheelchair led to tense chatter among them. As they rifled through our luggage and the wheelchair padding, we stood silently, lined up against the van. After twenty sweaty, high-stress minutes they gave up, likely only because another car pulled up behind us.

As we piled back into the van, everyone was muttering their relief, whispering small prayers of thanks or uttering deep sighs. I went straight for my Walkman and headphones. "Acoustic #3" on repeat. The best way to calm my emotions was by blocking out everything else but the uncomplicated, inviting notes of that simple song.

· · · · · · · · ·

I could no longer listen to the Goo Goo Dolls' song on repeat when I returned to Seattle after first seeing Deborah. Soothing Deborah's rejection called for something even more immersive: playing Pachelbel's Canon on the piano for hours on end. The bass line repeats the same eight notes throughout the entire piece. That reliable repetition kept me grounded. When I wasn't lost in that cyclical loop, I was having trouble holding regular conversations. I grew argumentative with my friends whose angered reactions and hot emotions (on my behalf) for the trip to Tennessee felt misplaced and deeply uncomfortable to me. I countered their sadness with fancy abstract reasons that didn't leave much room for argument.

"I'm just so sorry that she rejected you," they said.

"Well, for Black southerners, trauma is inherited," I'd pontificate in a professorial voice, "and poverty is inherited as a result. Deborah is poor. This does not also mean that she didn't love me or didn't want me." I'd continue in that safe, nonemotional education mode, teaching my friends about Dorothy Roberts, the author of *Shattered Bonds*, who viewed transracial adoption as another state-sanctioned way to dismantle Black families in America. Roberts contends that child-welfare policies reflected a political choice to address the startling rates of Black child poverty by punishing Black parents instead of tackling poverty's societal roots.[1]

"Perhaps Deborah was startled to realize that I was raised by white people and couldn't process all of that in a single moment," I surmised to myself and my friends, who may have tuned me out by this point. This smokescreen of the professorial version of myself was a necessary layer of protection for me in that moment. I was simply not yet ready to face the full weight of my emotions. And, while to some extent an avoidance strategy, digging into this research did increase my understanding of Deborah's situation.

Ever since reading the National Association of Black Social Workers' statement about transracial adoption being akin to racial genocide, I had wondered about the role race played from my birth mother's perspective. The 1970s were a time when racism and racist violence were daily occurrences: Jim Crow had been defeated in court but hadn't yet died in society; Martin Luther King Jr. had recently been assassinated. Racial segregation was still practiced, voting rights were still restricted for Black Americans in some areas of the country, and laws that prohibited interracial marriages were still on the books in the South (as well as in Delaware and Oklahoma). Black families were under attack on numerous facets of their daily life. It was the beginning of mass incarceration, which disproportionately impacted Black Americans, and the beginning of a national recession that hit Black men the hardest. Child protective services started to remove children of color from their homes at a higher rate than they removed white children. Deborah would have been in her late twenties and early thirties in this decade. Her early adulthood paralleling these difficult times. In 1985, when Deborah gave birth to me, perhaps she knew that Black people were losing their children to well-intentioned, color-evasive, loving white parents.

"Perhaps Deborah was eager to meet me, but was disappointed to learn that she was a victim in the latest strategy toward the deracination of the Black family?" I would say to my friends, who would look at me with big eyes. I could tell they wanted to say, "I'm sorry, Angela. This must be really hard." But my academic soliloquies did not leave room for any pity.

· · · · · · · · · ·

Tammy, a young Black mother of three, is a tragic example of the truth behind Dorothy Roberts's assertion that transracial adoption functions as a state-sanctioned dismantling of the Black family. In 2003, Tammy and her two children lived with her grandparents on a fixed income. She was often forced to choose between taking her kids to their doctors' appointments and working a shift to make enough money for food. When one child's ant bite turned into a staph infection and her other child's upper respiratory infection turned into pneumonia, child protective services moved in, charging Tammy with medical neglect and placing her kids in a foster home.

Tammy's children were adopted by a white couple in another state, who gained national attention in 2014 after posting a photo of their Black adopted son hugging a white police officer with tears streaming down his face during a Black Lives Matter march. Set against the backdrop of Michael Brown's death and the police officer's subsequent acquittal, the photo was received as an ode to world peace and proof that transracial adoption is a picture-perfect antidote to saving neglected children. Not only did Tammy's children now have a "stable" home, with two parents who could afford to take them to their doctors' appointments, but the parents also seemed to be allies in justice for Black lives in America. Indeed, the caseworker used this photo as evidence that the white couple could adopt another Black child, writing, "The family takes every opportunity to celebrate the children's ethnic heritage."[2]

But the reality was far from stable. In 2018, the news broke that the adoptive parents committed a murder-suicide by driving their SUV off a California cliff with their six children inside. Investigations later showed that there had been six documented reports of abuse against their adopted children, including withholding food, physical punishment, and harsh discipline tactics, but none of these reports resulted in any substantial action.[3]

The extreme nature of Tammy's children's story is on the rarer side, but it paints a clear picture of a child welfare system that assumes Black children must be saved from the social ills of their culture, which is quick to believe the glossy, social media posts that depict wokeness.

Becca Heller, the executive director of the International Refugee Assistance Project, spoke about how child welfare systems have become so bureaucratic that no one individual is forced to take responsibility for tragedies like this: "The brilliance of the system is that their job has been siphoned off in such a way that maybe what they see on a day-to-day basis seems justified. But when you add up all the people 'just doing their job' it becomes this crazy, terrorizing system."[4]

I began to realize that Deborah's rejection of me was a culmination of decisions made by numerous people in a fractured child welfare system. I started to acknowledge that I was angry about being rejected, but my anger wasn't really toward Deborah at all. It was toward all the faceless individuals in the child welfare system who directed the course of my life away from my being able to know my biological mother and who neglected to provide resources to help her heal.

Ultimately, I sympathized with Deborah's reaction. I must've startled her when I showed up at her door without any confirmation that she'd received my initial letter. And I showed up with a posse of middle-class white people, standing with a man whom she hadn't seen for twenty-five years! Of course, she'd be defensive.

As I sympathized more with Deborah, I found myself lost in my imagination, back in the familiar territory of the Ghost Kingdom, conjuring a woman I was still not able to know in real life. In my Ghost Kingdom, Deborah was a wise woman who was hep to the ways power is distributed away from poor people like her. In my Ghost Kingdom, Deborah's rejection of me was actually a rejection of colonization. Her actions had nothing to do with whether she loved me or not. In fact, maybe Deborah loved me so much that she wanted to prevent me from learning those hard truths. Maybe she wanted to protect me from the realities of being poor and Black in America. I thought back to a comment

Jesse had made in the Adoptee Lounge in Seattle: "My parents tell me, 'Your mom loved you so much she placed you for adoption.'" I sought evidence to confirm what I wanted to believe about Deborah, and this sounded pretty good.

In his book *My Grandmother's Hands*, Resmaa Menakem writes, "If something is hysterical, then it is usually historical. If one's reaction to a situation has more energy than it normally would, then it likely involves energy from ancient historical trauma that has lost its context."[5] Deborah's response seemed hysterical. Granted, she was not screaming or over-wrought with external emotion, but a denial of one's own child seemed to fit Menakem's description of a body that was experiencing unmetabolized trauma from the past.

I employed the support of a genealogist to look deeper into my an-cestry. She found a census report that stated that my great-grandmother died from "pneumonia." However, the genealogist knew that there was often more to the story than what a census provides. She taught me that in the 1920s it was common practice for a woman seeking an abortion to be denied medical care until she "confessed." The result was that fifteen thousand women a year died from botched abortions or "pneumonia" as they recorded it.[6]

Linking this information to the fact that my ancestors were brought to the South from Ghana in the 1600s helped me to detach from the sting of personal rejection. Perhaps Deborah wasn't rejecting me, but she was rejecting the opportunity to finally face the traumatic moment when she realized that she wouldn't be able to keep me. Perhaps she was rejecting the reminder of the trauma her grandmother endured. Perhaps she was rejecting the trauma that remains in her blood passed down from her ancestors who came over from West Africa. Maybe the mere sight of me with my white mother provoked Deborah's deep and ancestral feelings about white people and the complex interdependence on those whose ancestors had inflicted slavery, genocide, racial exclusion laws, legal seg-regation, and other methods of trying to "adopt" folks of color into the mainstream without fundamentally changing the way the power structures favor white people.

I felt the truth of all of this in my bones. I knew, on a deep level, that this version of my Ghost Kingdom had little in common with previous forays during my teen years into who my parents might be. This was real. And yet, as my left hand methodically tapped the bass line to Pachelbel's Canon in D and tears streamed down my cheeks, I also knew these insights into history and racism did not heal the place in me that Deborah's rejection shattered. This pain cannot be intellectually rationalized away.

. . . .

Nancee, the Lay's-eating, M&Ms-loving adoptee with pink streaks in her blond hair, never believed her adoption caused her any trauma. When I first met her, she introduced herself by saying, "I'm not one of those adoptees that thinks very much about adoption. It just didn't really impact me. In fact, I'm probably one of the most well-adjusted adoptees you've ever met." She went on to tell me how even the worst setbacks in life, of which she'd had many as an adult, couldn't hold her back. Her positivity and intense work ethic were certainly admirable. Still, in all Nancee's protestations I heard an underlying yearning that many adoptees do not see or that they struggle to reckon with: their perpetual desire to be successful, to be remarkable, to prove that we are worthy. Though it is hard to acknowledge, I believe this need stems from the initial rejection of our birth mothers. I pushed Nancee a bit to see if she wanted to consider this with me at all.

"Have you ever thought that your need to overachieve could be linked to a fear of abandonment?" I asked. "What do you think we learned in the minutes and hours after losing our mothers?" I was prepared for pushback, both because Nancee was so certain of her lack of trauma and because the Blank Slate theory still has its claws in the adoption industry.

The Mitchells were curious about the Blank Slate theory, too. After adopting Heather's baby, they emailed me saying, "We read that babies can feel connected to their biological mother, even if they were transitioned to their new family immediately after being born. Do you believe this?"

"Yes," I responded in an email along with a link to Nancy Verrier's book *The Primal Wound*. This book fuels intense debate. The theory holds that "severing the connection between the infant and biological mother [through adoption] causes a primal wound which often manifests in a sense of loss (depression), basic mistrust (anxiety), emotional and/or behavioral problems and difficulties in relationships with significant others . . . affect[ing] the adoptee's sense of self, self-esteem and self-worth throughout life."[7] Although there are plenty of people who disagree with the primal wound theory, the book is often lauded as the bible for adoptees because of the way it highlights potential impacts of loss and separation.

Nancee was surprisingly open to my inquiry. Although Nancee's adoptive parents loved her and doted on her in the same way they did their other children, she began recalling stories throughout her life where she'd felt unlovable and unworthy. She discovered that at a young age she became a chameleon, trying to be whatever or whomever people needed her to be. To this day, she realized that she never puts herself in situations where she will have to rely on someone else in order to avoid being disappointed when they don't show up, when they drop the ball, or when they flat out reject her. I relate to Nancee in this way. As she began attending the Adoptee Lounge, she realized she was not alone. Many adoptees in the Lounge also identified with Nancee's people-pleasing behaviors.

Not long after we met, Nancee attempted to reconnect with her birth mother. It was not an easy decision for her to make but, as with all things in her life, she dove in with gusto, finding her mother in record time. She wrote a beautiful email telling her birth mother about her life and requesting connection. A few weeks later she called, a hard edge to her voice as she told me she'd received a response: "I don't want to have anything to do with you. I put you up for adoption for a reason. I hope you've had a good life."

There is an email that has been sitting Nancee's draft folder for years. It's a response to her birth mother. When she read it aloud to me, I winced at the pain in her words. In the letter, Nancee is essentially selling herself, offering reasons for her birth mom to reconsider. "I'm educated. I'm a good mom. I have a beautiful son." It's a plea for acceptance with a painful underbelly of fear of not being good enough. I'm not sure if Nancee will ever send this response. Each adoptee manages the confusing and often lifelong pain of rejection in different ways.

When I was inside Deborah's uterus, I heard her voice, I tasted what she ate, I ingested her cigarette smoke and became familiar with her deep, gunky cough. I got to know her intimately, but she may have not even felt me kicking inside of her. Or maybe she did feel me, but she ignored me. Maybe, like Nancee's birth mother, she simply didn't want anything to do with me. I was the unfortunate side effect of sex. That's it.

I continued playing Canon in D for hours and hours, day after day. And little by little, with each note of the bass line and each new conversation I had with myself wondering why she rejected me, took me a tiny bit closer to the pain, a tiny bit closer to sympathy and understanding, a tiny bit closer to "what comes next?"

CHAPTER 10

SURVIVOR'S GUILT

CHILD STUDY—Part II: *Family History*

Deborah had four children prior to the birth of Angela. The first is a son, Timothy, who is 10 years old. James is 7 years old and stands 4' 2" in height. He is of a large bone structure and has black hair. Carolyn is age 3. She is of medium complexion and has brown eyes. She has not yet entered school. The fourth child was a female born on January 19, 1984. This child was adopted to another family. All of Angela's siblings are half siblings.

I'D READ THESE words hundreds of times over the years, each time hoping that more facts about my siblings would magically appear. *Where were they? What do they look like? Do they play sports? Why wasn't I adopted into the same family as my sister?*

The last question puzzled me the most. The adoption agency had told my parents that my half-sister's adoptive parents knew that I was in foster care, but they weren't interested in adopting me. My mom sent a letter to the adoption agency and asked that they forward it to my half-sister's family, asking if she and I could be pen pals; they refused. And while this hurt, it felt different from a rejection. It was perplexing. I simply could not make sense of their desire to keep me from knowing my sister. This sister became known as "Maya" in my imaginary, alternate reality. She was named after the tenacious and powerful survivor Maya Angelou.

My Ghost Kingdom was very active imagining the life my biological siblings must have had with Deborah. I imagined that they lived in a small apartment, and although the fridge was often empty and the heat didn't work in the winters, love bonded them together. I imagined Deborah panhandled on the corner while Carolyn, Tim, and James were at school. I pictured her standing on the corner, with a smile so big that passersby couldn't help but to be fueled by their empathy to support her.

The People Could Fly by Virginia Hamilton was one of my favorite picture books in childhood. It told fanciful stories of enslaved people in the southern United States who had the ability to fly away using their imagination as the tool to be set free. In the book, the characters preserved their culture, while being forced to adopt European ideals and standards, through oral folktales and storytelling. The book was accompanied by an audio cassette with James Earl Jones's narration. As I listened and turned the pages, leafing through the whimsical artwork, I envisioned my sister, Carolyn, sitting between Deborah's legs as she braided her hair. In my imagination hair days happened every Saturday. Deborah would slather Vaseline between the braids and tell Carolyn stories like the ones I was reading. She'd teach Carolyn about how enslaved people braided intricate cornrow patterns in each other's hair to communicate routes to freedom. Even though I knew this tale could be folklore, I longed to learn about the resiliency of my ancestors directly from my biological mother. I was longing to be the one sitting between Deborah's legs, hearing stories about our ancestors.

· · · · · · · · · ·

Brielle, fifteen, was adopted from Ethiopia and lives in a small town in Maine with her white mom. Our monthly hourlong mentorship sessions are the only time she gets to share all her thoughts related to Blackness and adoption. Brielle's words came out like water from a fire hose. It seemed she was always nervous that there wouldn't be enough time for all of her thoughts. She told me about the precarious position she was in earlier in the week when her teacher asked the class—all white students except for her—who founded the Black Lives Matter movement. She felt as though everyone was staring at her, waiting for her to answer. It was as though people expected her to speak for the entire race.

When Brielle and I first began meeting, I commented about how we both had 4C hair. She looked at me as though I was speaking a different language. The term "4C hair," which I taught her as I introduced her to a whole new world of natural hair textures, refers to tightly coiled, kinky strands that have a tight zig-zag pattern that is sometimes not discernible to the naked eye.

Brielle and I would talk about what leave-in conditioner to try, what a protective style is, and how to twist her hair. She began asking her mom questions about her hair, which led to her mom scrolling through endless Instagram videos of white adoptive parents gloating about learning to cornrow their Black children's hair. Brielle did not want to let her mom do this to her, feeling it would make her seem like a guinea pig, a test subject.

"It seems kinda show-offy, like they're just trying to show off how woke they are," Brielle said to me.

It was an astute comment. Resources for white parents of Black or biracial children are becoming more prevalent because of the movements relating to Black liberation in the face of white beauty standards. White parents are gradually learning how they are unwittingly reinforcing Eurocentric beauty standards and thwarting Black and biracial children from developing a sense of pride in their Blackness. There are quite a few books by white people about doing their Black children's hair, including one book called *Chocolate Hair Vanilla Care*—a title that hearkens back to the ways white people often use food to describe Black people. In the book, the author describes herself as an "afro-whisperer";[1] however, in the years following, she stepped back from that description and began encouraging white adoptive parents to learn about caring for Black hair from Black people. In a searing article titled "Eating the [M]Other," Richey Wyver discusses how "descriptions of race differences can also come in the form of food race metaphors: for example, 'chocolate skinned'; 'almond eyed'; 'coffee colored.' These metaphors function as coded racial markers that, in signifying desire and affection, are accepted as being positive race language." The article utilizes bell hooks's classic essay "Eating the Other: Desire and Resistance" to explore this phenomenon, arguing that this language "also gives [white adoptive parents] a claim to a connection with the adoptee that goes beyond biology."[2]

I'd given speeches at camps for transracial adoptive families where they hire Black hairstylists to come and teach white parents about how to do their children's hair. At one camp, a white woman told me, "I remember walking into a Black beauty supply store for the first time when my daughter was just three years old. I was nervous and felt completely out of place and if it hadn't been for a wonderful friend of mine who happens to be Black, I probably would've walked out quicker than I walked in." That parent reached in her pocket for her phone and showed me countless photos of every angle of her child's hair. She stated, "I'm so glad I've figured out how to do her hair, because it's hard parenting my children under the Black gaze." Several parents turned to her to share stories of times when they felt they were being chastised by Black strangers because of the state of their child's hair, saying that they felt the Black community was always watching them like a hawk. Another parent entered the conversation with a different angle, explaining that she felt gratitude for the Black people in her community who showed genuine support and care, even offering to teach the mother how to care for the hair. That mother spoke confidently about the benefits both she and her child have gained from these conversations, which spun into genuine relationships.

Brielle toed the line between advocating for herself against microaggressions while also showing respect to her mom. She shared numerous examples with me when we spoke each month. I suggested Brielle share with her mother how that was making her feel and asked if she'd take her to get her hair done by a professional. Brielle was excited to try this, hoping that her mom would feel relieved of any pressure. A month after that discussion, she told me that her mother scheduled an appointment to InHAIRitance Curl Spa.

To prepare for the appointment, we scrolled through hundreds of pictures of people who had her similar hair texture on Pinterest. Brielle had lots of opinions on each style and as usual, our conversation was fast paced. She volleyed questions at me faster than I had time to think of strategic responses to help her better understand her own identity rather than just telling her what I think. She decided to make a list of topics she hoped to talk about with her hairstylist:

Is it okay for Black people to use the N-word?

Is it okay for white people to use the N-word if they are reading it in a book? Or quoting a song?

Do you ever have to deal with people touching your hair without consent?

Do you ever wish you had silky, straight hair like white people?

I could feel Brielle's rising excitement; it was palpable. I was happy for her and proud that she took the step to be honest with her mom and ask for what she wanted.

My first time in a Black hair salon was when I was just four years old. I got my first chemical relaxer. My mom had found the lone Black hairstylist in Bellingham and asked her to help her understand what to do with my hair. That hairstylist suggested a relaxer, which was very common in those days—and had been since the 1950s. While damaging to hair, these harsh chemical treatments were the only way to make hair like mine, with tight curls and course texture, resemble anything close to the straight locks that most closely resemble Eurocentric beauty ideals. Trusting her advice, and with few other sources to ask, my mom sat by as she watched me squirm in my seat as the chemicals burned my hair into straight formation.

I repeated this painful process with at-home hair relaxer kits. I did this until college when I swapped out the relaxers for wigs and weaves, until finally, when I was in my twenties, I did a Big Chop. I chopped off all of my chemically damaged hair allowing for new hair to grow in, revealing my natural curls. Being bald was an empowering public embrace of my Blackness. A rejection of the European, bone-straight hairstyles that are so often synonymous with what it means to be beautiful in America. Despite being viewed as masculine, being called angry, and condescendingly being told "don't worry, it'll grow back fast," the Big Chop helped me to begin loving my natural kinks and exploring other Afrocentric hairstyles.

Brielle tells me that InHAIRitance Curl Spa is three hours away in Montreal, Canada. The distance doesn't bother Brielle, who hopes that making the trip will provide her with a sense of belonging that has always been out of reach. But when we sign in for our next session, Brielle is crestfallen. Her hair appointment was canceled due to COVID-19 pandemic restrictions that precluded Americans from crossing the border into Canada.

"I seriously doubt I'll ever get to have a true Black experience!" she said as tears flowed down her face. "I guess I'll just have to keep being seen as the exotic Black girl." Sniffling, she offered examples of how she felt being used to fill diversity quotas. The fact that she was often chosen to be the lead in the play, put in the center of class photos, and placed on the front page of the school's website only support her belief. "I hope that's not true though. I hope it's because of how much I practice and the effort I put into everything I do." She shifted her eyes from the screen to pick at her fingernail. "But being the only Black person at school, it's hard to know. It's like I'll probably feel like this forever!"

Brielle always ends our sessions by making sure I know she loves her mom and is grateful for everything she's given her. The way she soothes herself by minimizing her need for racial representation and replacing it with the materialistic gains that are assumed to come with adoption reminds me of myself.

Christmastime provides my most vivid memories of this. I'd lay in bed on Christmas Eve eager for the morning to arrive. Our home was converted into a winter wonderland; "Santa" left six to eight gifts for me and also for each of my siblings, foreign exchange students, foster siblings, or whoever was living in our house at the time. When tallied up, it equated to about fifty or sixty gifts under the tree. The tree itself was twenty feet tall, stretching from the main floor up to the second floor under the twenty-five-foot cathedral ceiling and jerry-rigged together with wires and hooks in the wall to keep it from falling over. We each opened gifts individually, stopping for food breaks, testing out new toys, or changing out of our pajamas to take a family photo. Interspersed throughout the day were thoughts of my biological siblings, whose Christmas looked very different from mine in my Ghost Kingdom. Like Brielle, I thought "I probably wouldn't have all of this if I wasn't adopted."

> Would I have questioned the legitimacy of Black folklore if I was raised by Black people?
>
> Would Brielle have to drive three hours for her first hair appointment as a high schooler if she was raised in the Black community?

The gains and losses of our transracial adoptions played like a metronome in my mind. A constant hum of cognitive dissonance.

· · · · · · · · · ·

The whir of the blender woke me from a restless sleep. It's unusual for Bryan to be awake before me, though it had been more common since we returned from Chattanooga. While I'd mostly been able to function just fine in my job and with friends, Bryan saw the small indicators of struggle. The poor sleep. The hours at the piano. The edge to my voice. Many mornings I'd awake, not to my usual energetic desire to start my day but to him gently offering me a cup of tea or a smoothie to help get me going.

I was barely a few sips into the delicious smoothie when he burst out, "Have you thought about trying to find your siblings?" We'd discussed it many times, of course. While Deborah held a special and unique place in my identity, my curiosity and longing for my siblings was real as well. Knowing that Timothy, James, and Carolyn were most likely still in Chattanooga, most likely on social media, made it seem like they wouldn't be hard to find. I'd hoped to connect with Deborah and reach out to them through her. But since that door had been painfully and unceremoniously closed, I'd lost momentum in finding my siblings.

The look on Bryan's face, his hopefulness, and his earnest fervor to keep piecing together what was missing from my puzzle were enough to awaken something in me that had lain dormant for a few months. I couldn't know Deborah. Not now. But perhaps I could still know my biological siblings. Perhaps that could help fill the void. I smiled. "Let's do it."

We dug into searches using the information we had from the Child Study. I used different searches to link Deborah Johnson to her relatives. Finding names that I believed were her brothers and sisters, I made my way back to Facebook, typed in those names, and without hesitation wrote them direct messages.

Hello, I was wondering if you knew or are related to Deborah Johnson? I think we may be related. Last summer I came to Chattanooga and met whom I believe to be my birth mother: Deborah Johnson (DOB: 3/11/1954). I was really excited to meet her however she denied giving birth to me. I do think she is my birth mother, but don't want to press it. So, I'm now reaching out to see if we might be related. I'm not meaning to scare anyone, and do not want any money from you. I just want to get to know my family somehow.

Within hours I had a response from Belinda Johnson, whom I would come to learn was my biological aunt.

Angela, I am blown away. I never knew Deborah had another daughter, but you know too many details about all of us for this to be a joke. Deborah denied you last year? God help us all. I'm so sorry that she did that to you. I have tears in my eyes, and I just want to say I'm sorry. Please call me.

I called Belinda right away. My hands shook as I picked up my cell phone. I felt a familiar tightness in my chest with the first ring. I knew from Belinda's kind and open email response I should expect kindness from her. But my body seemed stuck on the street outside Deborah's house, waiting for the sting. My fears melted away with Belinda's first greeting, "Oh baby doll, it is such a joy to hear your voice!" She was emotional, clearly feeling a mix of confusion, sadness, and joy, but she wanted to help me and extend the best possible welcome she could. I could tell there was decades of sibling tension between her and Deborah. I felt drawn to her and accepted by her in ways I'd hoped with Deborah. This realization both encouraged and saddened me. Before we hung up, Belinda shared the names, phone numbers, and Facebook pages of my siblings.

I went to Carolyn's Facebook page first. The person I knew as my three-year-old sister was now a twenty-nine-year-old woman with two children who went by the nickname Nay-Nay. I stared at her Facebook profile, taking in her every feature. She was wearing a bright yellow shirt, her skin was a bit darker than mine, and her eyebrows were thicker. I couldn't believe I was looking at my sister. I scrolled through every Facebook post and every photo that she'd ever posted. I looked for people who commented regularly, trying to get a sense of who her friends were. I found James's Facebook page and was excited to see that he'd posted photos at the Oklahoma City Thunder NBA game. It was overwhelming to suddenly have Timothy, James, and Nay-Nay's names, phone numbers, and Facebook pages. I couldn't remember if Belinda said that she'd give them a heads-up about me or not. It was possible that my phone calls to Timothy, James, and Nay-Nay might be a shocking surprise to them, too.

During our first FaceTime, I was so excited I could hardly contain myself. I know I talked too fast and asked way too many questions in rapid succession. I felt like an investigative reporter finally able to get to the truth behind my Ghost Kingdom.

Nay-Nay spoke in a measured voice, which was much calmer than mine, almost tearful. "I've always wanted a sister. I can't believe I have one. We have a lotta catching up to do. I can't wait till we get girl time, just me and you and a glass of wine."

Our first conversation covered the small-talk territory. Both of us were feeling each other out, wanting to get to know each other, but not wanting to come on too strong. It was the ultimate test in making a good first impression, which led to pregnant pauses and the looks common on a first date. I broke the ice first, delving in with a deeper question.

"How did Deborah hide her pregnancies from you?" I asked. "I know you would've been just three years old when I was born, but do you remember her being pregnant?"

Nay-Nay was quiet. My heart started pounding so loud I was sure she could hear it. *Had I overstepped? What kind of pain was my question bringing up for her?* Finally, she looked up with a sadness in her eyes. "Deborah is a very complicated person. She's lived a hard life. I don't remember much about my childhood. I stayed at my grandma's house a lot until she died when I was twelve years old. I didn't see our brothers much, either."

I was stunned. Over the nearly three decades of making up stories about my biological siblings, it never crossed my mind that although she wasn't adopted, she may not have been raised by our biological mother either.

Nay-Nay went on to explain that after her grandmother died, she didn't return to live with Deborah. Instead, she found a new home with Esme and Esther, two of her classmates. She met them at her school bus stop and remembers staying the night at their homes every day after that. Esme and Esther's parents made sure that Nay-Nay got to school; they signed forms for her to go on school outings and came to treat her as another daughter. Others helped raise Nay-Nay, too. She remembers one teacher who discreetly slipped a hundred-dollar bill in her pocket from time to time to make sure she had some money. She spent holidays with her teachers, even Christmas, which happened to be her birthday, too. There were long stretches when Nay-Nay didn't know where Deborah was.

In sharing her story, Nay-Nay often said, "I don't really know how I survived." She had worked at a grocery store since she was fifteen years old. By seventeen, Nay-Nay got her own apartment by doctoring her birth certificate. She was born in 1981 but changed the number 1 to make it look like she was born in 1980. As Nay-Nay shared details about her life, my questions turned from intense curiosity to worry.

Who took you to your annual doctor appointments?
Who taught you how to ride a bike? Drive a car?

I learned James and Timothy had similarly fragmented lives in which Deborah was not a constant for them either. The three older siblings all knew about each other and saw each other from time to time at family gatherings. Nay-Nay wasn't sure how much Timothy and James lived together growing up or if, like her, they bounced around community and family. None of them knew about our other sister either.

I thought about my life in comparison. While Nay-Nay was floating from home to home, I was stable and loved in a big house with lots of siblings. While Nay-Nay was getting money from random teachers for school field trips, I was playing AAU basketball and traveling to games throughout the state. Nay-Nay sneezed many times throughout our conversation and rubbed her eyes repeatedly, which made me wonder if she had received consistent medical care like I did. My weekly allergy shots, though annoying, helped keep my asthma controlled and allowed my family to keep the emotional support cat for my siblings. Although my hearing aids cost thousands of dollars, they were covered by Tennessee's Adoption Support program since I was adopted through foster care. I never went without them. If I'd not been adopted and had grown up as Nay-Nay did, I might not have been afforded all the access to the medical care that I'd received. I'd grown up feeling jealous about the life I assumed Nay-Nay lived, however I was quickly realizing my assumptions were woefully inaccurate. I felt like a brick had formed in my stomach, a new kind of guilt that I suddenly felt very sharply. This feeling was reinforced by comments from my newfound Aunt Belinda, who said "God has blessed you with the better end of the deal. You see, 'round here, none of us got no material things; all we got is each otha. We are all poor, with no money, but we do got love. But you lucky. I see that you got both."

After my conversations with Nay-Nay and Belinda, I couldn't shake that brick in my belly. I had a constant nagging guilt. As usual, I turned to academic research, music, and, in this case, my mom, Bryan, and my therapist. Soon I had a name for what I was feeling: survivor's guilt.

The term was originally created to describe holocaust survivors. Typically, we think about survivor's guilt as referring to the emotional stress experienced by someone who has survived a car accident when another person in the same car died. But I was experiencing it as I compared my life to Nay-Nay's. Did I have a better life? I couldn't shake the question even though I know it was unanswerable. I longed to know Nay-Nay better, to understand her story more deeply. I longed to get past this immense survivor's guilt to be able to truly know Nay-Nay as my sister. After a few months of getting to know each other remotely, I invited Nay-Nay to Washington State to visit me. The night before her flight, she texted me a photo of three stilettos, "Which heels should I wear on the plane?" she asked. "I want to make sure I look on point if I run into any celebrities!" I chuckled, initially thinking she was joking, but her next text reminded me of our different upbringings.

Nay-Nay and I continually sought out proof of our likeness, but evidence of our differences seemed to pop up in every conversation. In Nay-Nay's world, travel and airplanes were experiences for the rich and famous. In my world, airplanes and airports were a nuisance, a necessary hassle in order to reach the actual experience or destination. I ended up explaining to Nay-Nay how traversing through security, the maze of airport wings, and long bathroom lines and weaving among stressed-out passengers all while shuffling the luggage were good reasons to dress comfortably. We talked through the sensation of liftoff and touchdown, including how bringing a pack of gum might be helpful in case she felt any pressure and needed to pop her ears. I was uncomfortably aware of my economic privilege as I spoke of the luxury of air travel in the same tone that many people use to describe the stress of planning a destination wedding.

Nay-Nay touched down in Bellingham, Washington, exhausted from two connecting flights, layovers in Atlanta and Seattle, and traveling across two time zones. Seeing each other in the flesh was intoxicating. We'd met before, in Chattanooga, but we were surrounded by lots of people and didn't get much one-on-one time. I thought again about Resmaa Menakem's *My Grandmother's Hands*:

> When two or more unfamiliar bodies first encounter one another, each body tends to either relax in recognition or constrict in self-protection. This happens quickly, automatically, and often unconsciously. Typically, each body goes briefly on alert while its lizard brain discerns, ASAP, whether the other body is safe or dangerous. In an instant, it scans hundreds of clues to make that determination: the other body's size, posture, clothing, speed of approach; what the body is saying or doing; the vibrations it seems to be giving out; the expression on the person's face; and so on. One shortcut the lizard brain uses to make this determination is by asking, how closely does this body match mine?[3]

The resemblance between Nay-Nay and me was nothing compared to Sandy and me. But I felt we matched in a different, more elemental way. Something in us fit together, despite our many, many differences.

We made our way to my parents' Victorian blue, green, and purple home, where my mom was anxiously awaiting us. This is the home I lived in for my high school years and where my parents became empty nesters. It's immaculate. The rosewood flooring gleams as though it had just been polished. The marble countertops hold beautiful bowls containing freshly picked tomatoes and raspberries that were grown in my parents' bountiful garden. My high school room, with the large window seat bed, white shutters, and built-in shelving all around, still had remnants of my childhood and looked like a storybook picture. Touring the house with Nay-Nay I felt both proud and somehow embarrassed, the first of many "brick in my belly" moments that would come and go throughout Nay-Nay's trip to Bellingham.

After a couple days of exploring Bellingham, Nay-Nay and I were sitting at a restaurant next to a white woman with cornrows in her hair. "You should know that people culturally appropriate Black people a lot here in the Northwest," I said in an effort to explain my fellow townspeople. Having learned about Nay-Nay's tendency toward positivity, I'd expected her to respond with some form of *cultural appropriation is the highest form of flattery*–type response, but she surprised me by saying, "You're lucky to be a high yella growing up in a place like this."

I took an especially large bite of my sandwich to buy myself a bit of time. I rifled through the recesses of my brain, trying to locate the definition of this unfamiliar phrase. But nothing was coming to mind. It was a moment where I feared she'd view me differently if I admitted that I didn't know what she meant.

"Thank you," I replied, trying to summon a confidence to make it seem like I was responding correctly. Nay-Nay didn't say anything back. We moved on with our conversation. Later that evening I looked up the term and learned that it refers to Black people who have lighter complexions or "yellow" undertones. But I wasn't sure why she'd think it was especially lucky to be that way growing up in Bellingham. The next day, I felt a panic rising in my throat, and the shame of self-doubt creeping in as I feared my new biological sister would think I had a bad case of internalized racism. I thought that I'd bring up her comment, still not quite admitting that I didn't know the term yesterday, but I wanted to understand why she said this.

"Yesterday you said I was lucky to be a lighter-skinned Black person. Why was that?"

Nay-Nay explained that my light skin tone puts white people at ease. "People know that you're Black, but they don't second-guess your qualifications because you're a light-skinned Black." She shrugged. "You'd totally pass the Brown Paper Bag Test." She was right. Again, I was uncomfortably aware of how different my life was from Nay-Nay's, this time due to a terrible practice of hierarchy based on relative skin tone.

The Brown Paper Bag Test was used as the barometer to assess Black people's "acceptability" because the color—halfway between black and white—was seen as the ideal shade for a Black person's skin. In his 1996 book, *The Future of the Race*, Henry Louis Gates Jr. described the practice, saying "Some of the brothers who came from New Orleans held a *bag party* . . . a bag party was a New Orleans custom wherein a brown paper bag was stuck on the door. Anyone darker than the bag was denied entrance."[4] This extended to institutions like movie theaters, grocery stores, and schools, and this form of prejudice also dictated whether someone would be hired for a job. It was a practice that ended in the 1950s, but as Nay-Nay was alluding to, the attitudes that surround this practice are still ever present. This belief has more or less become unconscious because of how deeply ingrained it is in American life. To this day, dark-skinned women are less likely to be married than lighter-skinned women.[5] Darker-skinned women are given longer prison sentences than high yellas,[6] and dark-skinned girls are more likely to be suspended from school.[7]

After learning about this term, I was embarrassed about what Nay-Nay must have thought about my answer. If only I'd been raised in the Black community, I wouldn't be so naive about my own culture, I thought. I felt deracinated. I felt like I was pulled up by the roots. Although its origins referred to literal plant roots, the phrase has taken on a second, metaphorical meaning about removing anyone or anything from its native roots or culture. Typically, when we transplant or deracinate plants, we do it very carefully and slowly and are advised to bring some of the native soil with the plant when placing it in the new location. And even when we do this, we know that some of the plants won't take root and will die. Or some will need extra tending. I wish I'd been transplanted with a bit of native soil. I wish I'd been adopted with Nay-Nay. I wish Nay-Nay could've been adopted with me. I wish we'd had all the economic benefits of my life but with the depth of understanding and Black identity that came with Nay-Nay's life.

Spending a week with Nay-Nay brought me to a whole new level in facing the reality of my adoption and how it had catapulted me up the socioeconomic ladder from the life I was born into, the life that Nay-Nay had. Survivor's guilt was now a near constant companion as I could not stop comparing my growing up with Nay-Nay's. I'm aware that "comparison is the thief of joy." I know this not simply because Teddy Roosevelt said so, but because I can taste it. It's bitter. So bitter that I can hardly speak aloud those words: *compared to Nay-Nay's life, I had it better.*

This comparison is a distinctly different experience than when we compare our lives to those shiny Instagram influencers who look a thousand times happier than us. It's different because those lies can be muted by unfollowing someone on social media or talking to a good friend who reminds you that social media posts are just a highlight reel with filters. Comparing my adopted life to my biological sibling's reality doesn't have an easy off switch. I'm measuring myself against a reality that genuinely could have been if a couple different decisions had been made. And I'm so glad I grew up with life I did, while simultaneously longing for parts of Nay-Nay's life. I was reckoning with the painful and confusing fact that perhaps I truly was lucky to have escaped that life. *Were the losses that I'd experienced through adoption a moot point given the gains I'd received? Were the people who said, "You should be grateful" right?*

JaeRan Kim, a Korean adoptee and researcher, wrote, "Some days I have a hard time being able to say adoption is a good thing when I know so many people for whom it wasn't. Yet, I don't believe it's better to grow up without family either. And some days it's terribly difficult to look in the mirror and be thankful for the blessings you feel you don't deserve."[8] The pain lies in the realization that it's more comforting to blame ourselves for things outside of our control than to accept that we truly were not responsible for the kind of life we were given.

My survivor's guilt felt reversed and twisted. Even with the harsh reality of her struggle for survival, I still somehow longed for Nay-Nay's life. Americans don't place a high value on Blackness, and we can barely bear to look poverty in the eye, which makes it difficult to express this desire. Yet there I was again, longing to be tended to, lovingly cared for, deeply integrated into my family of origin and my Black ancestral roots. It is frustrating to feel that there is no wrong to atone for or to make amends for. My version of survivor's guilt doesn't involve an accident or an atrocious genocide. My version involves an altruistic act by my adoptive parents and an attempt at survival for my biological mother. All of this leads me to have ongoing arguments with a faceless inner judge and to wrestle with a truth that doesn't fit within the confines of societal understanding.

Getting to know Nay-Nay has brought me so much joy. My heart flutters when I receive text messages from her and being able to be present for her wedding felt right. We both enjoy being in each other's presence and wish it could be a bit easier to get together in person. Nay-Nay and I send surprise gifts in the mail to each other, lovely reminders of how badly each of us wants to grow our relationship. Spending time with her ushered in a much longed-for sense of belonging. It has also brought a complicated and unresolvable experience of survivor's guilt that I'm not sure I will ever fully shake.

When Nay-Nay returned home to Tennessee, she wrote me an email. It said,

> Looking at the city where you grew up and seeing how your mom and dad raised you so beautifully took me aback. When we were going around town looking at the places you grew up and your high school and stuff, of course I had an inkling of thoughts like, if I had been raised here, what would I be doing, or how far in life would I be, what types of opportunities would I have been given? Of course, I had those thoughts. Your life is incredible. But if I'd had these opportunities, I wouldn't have my beautiful daughters. I don't hold myself in situations of the what ifs. I am just appreciative of life itself and am very happy that you had people who cared for you. I have always understood that God makes no mistakes.

CHAPTER 11

SANDY'S DEATH

"**A**NGELA? MY SWEET NIECE?" my aunt Pam said on the phone. "I just wanted to tell you, that I'm sittin' here wit' yo daddy, and he just took his last breath. He gone."

After colon cancer and then a stroke, Sandy had died. To him, he died a proud father. To me, he died almost as mysterious as he was when he was living. I'd known Sandy and his family for eight years, but my relationship with him never got very deep. Whenever I traveled to Chattanooga, I'd see him for just a short amount of time. The rest of his family was quite welcoming of me and my entire family. They sought to spend as much time as possible with me anytime I was in town. Aunt Pam and I share a similar body shape, so she would arrive with a bag of hand-me-down clothes for me every time we saw each other. My uncle Jay had a pool table in his basement where he invited me to come and hang out and shoot pool with him. In all of the wonderful hours I spent with them, rarely did anyone speak in great depth about Sandy's drug use or how he came to create this career of such a unique type of panhandling. The refrain was clear and simple. "Sandy the Flower Man is special. He was over the moon to find out he had a daughter. He tells everyone about you!"

. . . .

My mom, Bryan, and I flew to Chattanooga for the wake, funeral, and burial a couple weeks after Aunt Pam's phone call. We pulled up to the funeral home, where we saw some familiar cars in the parking lot. The funeral building was small, a one-story brick building just off a main thoroughfare. I'd never been to a wake before and had no idea what to expect. The nerves jostling around in my stomach got even jumpier as sounds of loud crying seeped out the funeral home doors. It was Aunt Pam. She was being consoled by my aunts and uncles who were standing in the lobby area, waiting to escort me into the main room in the funeral home. Sandy's siblings were dressed in suits or dresses. They greeted the three of us warmly, as though we had been part of their family for an eternity. My aunts and uncles guided me away from my mom and Bryan and up to Sandy's casket where we surrounded Sandy. They touched him, their hands outstretched toward his face, his shoulders. Some would lean down and kiss his face. Quiet sobs echoed off the walls. Aunt Pam reached over, offering another tearful hug, and pushed me close to the coffin. When I hesitated, she grabbed my arm and moved it toward Sandy. "Go ahead," she murmured. "Give him a hug." But I was frozen and could not make my arm or hand comply with her encouragement to touch Sandy's face or hug him. I felt desperately uncomfortable, afraid of offending these kind people who'd extended me such a warm welcome and openness. But I could not make myself touch Sandy's body.

After a few minutes, the family began to file out. I turned to go, but Uncle Jay touched my elbow and motioned that I should remain behind. "You take a special moment, honey," he said in a soothing tone. "Say goodbye to your daddy." Aunt Pam looked on approvingly. Everyone left, joining Bryan and my mom out in the lobby. It seemed that I was to be alone with Sandy to say my goodbyes. I stood somewhat shakily in front of Sandy's body. He was more of a yellowish tone, and I could tell someone had put a bit of makeup on his face to give him some color in his cheeks. They'd dressed him in a white suit with a red cumberbund. My eyes continued to wander, taking in his every feature and his lean frame. I'd guess that he barely weighed a hundred pounds. He seemed so delicate.

I stared at him, feeling less self-conscious to take in his every feature than I did when he was alive. It was still hard to believe that someone else in the world looked so like me. But my discomfort was palpable. I'd never been in the same room with a dead body before. Cremation was the standard practice for anyone I'd known that passed away. I had learned it was a more affordable option that was also better for the environment. I

YOU SHOULD BE GRATEFUL"   127

batted away my thoughts of wonder about why they wouldn't have chosen that route for Sandy.

Gratefully, I was only left alone with Sandy for a few minutes before the doors at the back of the room cracked open and the family filed back in for the public viewing. The jumpiness in my stomach began to calm down as we began the part of the day I expected would be more familiar.

The funeral service was elaborate and emotional. There was a buzz in the room. Everyone from the community greeted me with a reverence for being Sandy's daughter. Our reunion had been featured on the local news just eight years prior; it was a celebratory story for this local town celebrity. Because of his public persona, everyone knew that I was Sandy's only child, and they knew how proud he was of me. I felt their pride on Sandy's behalf. It felt wonderful, yet strange since I truly didn't know Sandy that well.

The hymns were reverent and lasted as long as they needed to last; the singer taking cues from the audience to determine whether to sing a verse again. I sat quietly. What a fittingly ironic reversal, I couldn't help but think. I wore all black and held my head low, not because I felt overwhelming sadness, but because that's how I'd been taught to behave at funerals. Here, though, the occasion felt joyous, even as I watched the open displays of sadness. People wore a mixture of red and black, an ode to Sandy's favorite color. They sang and yelled out spontaneously during the music, the speeches, the sermon—even during the eulogy. Again, I felt like a fish out of water. I was palpably aware of how separate I was from this culture. I tried to focus my mind on Sandy and the things people were saying about my biological father. But I couldn't stop my mind from constantly wandering to the other people in attendance; they had wholly embraced me. They didn't see me as a Black woman with an asterisk denoting that I wasn't really one of them. They welcomed me with open arms into the Bell family, into the city of Chattanooga, and into their church. For a moment, I was not self-conscious about my belonging. I knew I belonged.

There were flowers everywhere you looked. I was seated in the front row, just feet from Sandy's casket. Congregants formed a single-file line to walk up to the casket and pay their respects. After the first five people stopped to give me a long hug and squeeze my hand before returning to their pew, I realized that people weren't simply going to say what I'd expected to hear—"I'm sorry for your loss" repeatedly. Instead, people proceeded to tell me more stories about Sandy.

"Your daddy was a saint," one person said, wailing loudly.

"Your dad never asked me for a handout. He would say, 'I am short on money. Can I wash your windows?' or something like that. It was so respectful."

"Angela, I want you to know that Sandy wasn't just another panhandler. Some people may call him a 'hustler,' but he didn't beg. Sure, sometimes he would take sad wilting flowers from graveyards, but he turned them into joy and laughter for anyone who was lucky enough to receive one. What's wrong with that? You came from royalty."

I felt proud that my biological father was so beloved, that he could find a way to exist in tough circumstances, and that he created beauty in the world. But at the same time, I felt deeply sad for what could have been for Sandy and even sadder that I would not have the chance to know him better, that he didn't try harder to know me after meeting me. At this moment, I was somewhat grateful that I can't cry on command. My dry cheeks felt like the one bit of integrity I could preserve, the physical manifestation that reflected our actual relationship. In the limo from Olivet Baptist Church to Chattanooga National Cemetery, I learned that this was not called a funeral.

"This is yo father's homegoing! Sandy is going home!" my uncle corrected me, when I commented on how beautiful the funeral was. The homegoing legacy runs deep in Black communities. Enslaved people took solace in Christianity, finding stories about reaching the "promised land" and heaven to be an opportunity to be free from suffering. Many funeral parlors are proudly run by Black families who are highly regarded for the way they care for the dead. This is a result of the duties left to Black soldiers during the Civil War. It was their responsibility to remove the dead from the battlefields, keep those records, and preserve the bodies.

Many of the roads were shut down for the long procession of cars that snaked through the city from the church to the repast. *You came from royalty.* Only twenty people—including Sandy's siblings; my family (although only my mom and Bryan could make the trip); and Alison and John, my foster parents—were invited to the private military burial and the lowering of Sandy's casket into the ground. I was surprised to see my foster parents because I knew they didn't have a relationship with Sandy. They had been invited specifically to support me. In the chaos and exhaustion of the day, seeing my foster parents was incredibly grounding. When we hugged and my foster mother's blond hair fell across my back, the fear and worry that was twisted up in my body relaxed. Those preverbal memories imprinted somewhere within my body came flooding back. Even though my memories with Alison weren't easy to verbalize, my body responded as though I had known this person my entire life. It dawned on me that this was the feeling people thought I had with Sandy. But Sandy felt like an acquaintance who could be mistaken for my twin. Alison and John felt like people I'd known and loved my whole life. It felt like an attachment. They sat directly behind me and next to Bryan and my mom, as the bugler played "Taps."

In the limo ride over to the cemetery, my aunt Harriet let me know that I was going to be presented with the flag in honor of Sandy's military service. "You are his kin. You should get the flag," she said. I was overwhelmed and could not find the strength to accept that gift. I'd felt so loved by the whole community all day. A love that frankly surprised me after wading through a lifetime of fear that I wouldn't be accepted.

"Oh no. I can't possibly accept it," I said to Harriet. They could see how tender and fragile I was at that moment and didn't press me. "Let's just have them present it to you, okay?" I asked earnestly. They obliged but let me know that the flag was mine whenever I wanted it. The uniformed body bearers stood in front of Aunt Harriet, performing the folding and presentation of the flag, and said,

On behalf of the President of the United States, the United States Marine Corps, and a grateful nation, please accept this flag as a symbol of our appreciation for your loved one's honorable and faithful service.

I watched as Harriet outstretched her arms to accept the flag. I was glad that she stood in my place in that moment, as I was still trying to bat away the truth that I didn't even know where he served.

CHAPTER 12

I'M STILL LOOKING FOR MY BABY

A S LUCK WOULD have it—or some kind of universal providence—I was playing the piano when Deborah called me for the first time. I was just a few measures into my beloved Canon in D in our apartment that looked out at the Space Needle, when I saw my phone light up on the edge of the piano. I had painstakingly saved the phone numbers we'd called two years ago in the initial search for my birth mom, giving them contact names that reflected both my hope and uncertainty. When I glanced over and saw "Deborah Johnson" displayed on the screen, my heart skipped a beat.

Why is she calling me?

It had been over a year since Deborah had said, "I'm not the person you're looking for" in Chattanooga. Over two years since I'd sent her a letter that included my phone number and asked her to reach out. *Had she saved it all this time? Waiting for the courage to use it?*

"Bryan!" I yelled to the other room in a tone that got him moving immediately. As he rushed into the living room, I flashed the phone at him before sliding the little bar to answer it.

I'm not sure I got even a "hello" out past the lump in my throat before she started speaking.

"Angela, this is Deborah. Your birth mother."

My palms were instantly so sweaty I thought I'd drop the phone. I recognized her voice immediately. That voice was punctuated by deep gunky coughs that sounded like her lungs were revolting against her. No question, this was the woman who'd looked me in the eye and walked away just twelve months ago. No question, this was my birth mother.

"Hi! I'm so excited to speak with you!" I said in a voice that came out an octave higher than I'd wished. I cleared my throat and tried to prepare myself for what this conversation might entail. *Would all my questions be answered? Did she really, finally want to know me? Would she hang up mid-call if I offended her? Would this be the start of our relationship or the only time I'd hear her voice?*

"I'm sorry for how that went down last year," Deborah began, with a lingering hoarseness to her voice from a quick coughing fit, "but honestly, half of me want to know you, but half of me don't want to know you." Two years previously, when I'd first sent Deborah that letter, I couldn't have related to this. It would have hurt me so deeply, as I'd spent my whole life longing to know her. But now, after being welcomed into Sandy's family and feeling in my body all the complicated and confusing emotions that came with knowing my siblings, people who were meant to be my people but were, in some ways, foreign, I felt immediate empathy and understanding for Deborah's opening statement. Half of me thought of her as a stranger or a client at work, both of whom I always offer my complete attention and reserve judgment, extending empathy for the fact that I know very little about their lives. The other half of me remembered the pain of her rejection. I tried to allow both of those halves to be present at the same time. I knew I could offer kindness and empathy for Deborah, while not avoiding the truth.

I recorded our phone call, fearing, just like last year, that this might be the only true conversation I'd get to have with Deborah, and knowing that I'd want to listen and relisten to the conversation—not merely to understand the content but to just hear her voice, her deep, resonant, and powerful voice and that persistent rasp. I even wanted to hear the cadence of her coughing fits. I wanted to measure the space between sentences during those times when she couldn't find her thoughts. This was my mother. My flesh and blood. I wanted to know her. I treasured anything I could get.

"When you came to my door last year, I stared at you and thought about how those doctors lied to me," she went on. "They told me you would be a cripple. But instead, you looked just fine—that's no thanks to me, of course." I wanted to interrupt her and tell her that my disabilities aren't something that I hide in shame. I wanted to ask about that time around my birth. I wanted to tell her that I thought she was brave for all she had gone through. But I stopped myself, remembering that there is a consensus among adoption researchers that for many women the experience of relinquishing a child is fraught with intense feelings of grief, loss, shame, guilt, remorse, and isolation.

"Brave" is a word that the Mitchells used to describe Heather, the nineteen-year-old biological mother of the Mitchells' baby. In private, she told me how much she despised that word. One birth mother said, "People like to say, 'Oh you're a hero, you're so brave, you did such an amazing thing . . . ' but people have no clue how awful it is to live like this. It is true torture. I would take it back in a heartbeat. There should be strict laws requiring counseling for birth mothers, so they really understand what they are getting into."[1]

I managed to squeeze in a few affirmations for Deborah, letting her know that I now understood why she needed to reject me when I came to her home. I tried to reassure her that I wasn't mad at her and didn't harbor any hard feelings. But I don't think she was listening to me. I got the impression that if we were in person, she wouldn't be looking me in the eye. She was kind of talking past me.

"I've had strokes and seizures over the years, so I don't remember some things very well," Deborah said. "But when I was pregnant with you—or maybe it was the other girl—I was livin' outta my car." I noticed Deborah's tendency to mutter to herself quietly in between her louder, articulated sentences meant for me to hear. Sometimes I'd catch a few words. It sounded like she was trying to pull her thoughts together, to remember things that were eluding her. "That's the problem, too," she said loud and clear. "I don't know which one you are. I didn't name you or the other girl that got taken from me. I don't know if you know this or not, but I'm not just *your* birth mother. I had to give away two babies back then. I was starin' at you but couldn't figure out which one you were."

My mind raced as she spoke. Deborah's conversation style is meandering and can be hard to follow. She often interjects with self-deprecating language, which I hate, because I view self-deprecation as a form of verbal self-harm. If any of my mentees use this language, I typically counter it by asking, "Would you say this about a friend?" But it didn't feel right to shift into the familiar mentor role at that moment, so I stayed quiet and grabbed a towel to dry my sweaty palms. The more I stayed silent, the deeper Deborah went. It seemed that she had a lot to get off her chest. I got the feeling that this would be more of a monologue than a conversation. It seemed she had twenty-six years of stories, thoughts, and context that she wanted to tell me.

"I've been tortured by all of this. I didn't tell no one about you or the other one. No one but me knows how hard this has been." She cleared her throat, possibly holding back tears. I swallowed hard as well. "And then there you are, showing up seeing me in this condition, and you looking like you have had a perfect life. Nah, I ain't got no right to interfere with that," she said with force. "That's why I had to send you away."

Hearing Deborah speak made me question my steadfast assertion that I deserved to know my truth at all costs. My precarious position rested on two conflicting principles that remained inflexible my entire life. One is the fact that I deserve to know my own truth about my life. The other is that my birth mother deserves her privacy. It wasn't simply that I was curious to know Deborah. Curiosity is a shockingly inadequate word for my drive. My biological history is as much a part of my essential self as my limbs or senses, and to be deprived of the knowledge of my origins, ancestry, and people feels as though I've been maimed. But I couldn't help but wonder, as Deborah trailed off into a muttering soliloquy, if knowing my truth was more important than allowing my birth mother her privacy.

When should I interrupt and tell her that I've had a good life?

Does she even know that I grew up in Washington State?

Does she know that I play piano? Does she care to know?

"After you were born, I found a little place to live, and I didn't come out," she went on. "I locked myself in a little shack and didn't want to see no one."

Deborah didn't evoke any sense of shame or embarrassment when sharing about her life. She never bothered to pretty up her sentences or speak in fancy euphemisms. She had a careful southern gentleness: she would apologize before cussing, for example—and ask pardon for saying anything bad about anyone. But when it came to saying things that others might blush to say or try to avoid saying, she launched right in without any fuss, pivoting constantly between talking about me and whatever else she wanted to share.

Your daddy told me he couldn't have no kids. So, I don't know how you're here. It's selfish to keep a child you can't do any good for. I just had to take the hit.

After an hour of listening to her talk, one of my dreams came true. My simple dream to hear evidence that she remembered me. That she hadn't forgotten about me.

"Over the years, I've wondered where you were and what you were doing," Deborah muttered. My heart skipped a beat. These were the words I'd longed to hear for twenty-six years, but just as quickly as that dream was realized, it vanished with her next sentence: "But at the same time, I don't believe that you're the baby I had." My stomach dropped.

"I'm still looking for my baby," she concluded, and the fragile joy I'd felt began to crumble.

While my body felt that familiar pang of rejection, my brain understood what was happening, and I told myself firmly that this response is about Deborah, not me. I reminded myself that Deborah was stuck in the moment of her trauma immediately after my birth. She'd never gotten past it. She completely dissociated from my birth and since she didn't have any therapeutic support to make sense of my adoption, the fact that I'd grown up into an adult was incomprehensible to her. She could only see me as that baby they took away. She couldn't comprehend the woman I'd become. When trauma isn't fully integrated, it can stunt our emotional development. I decided to chime in, changing the subject and giving us both a break from this painful shift in the conversation.

"Deborah, did you know that my parents sent you photos of me every year?" I asked. She had no idea what I was talking about.

It is common and advised for adoptive parents to update their child's biological parent about how the child is doing. For some birth families, the level of openness is a factor in their selection of adoptive parents.[2] The preference is for communications to be conducted directly between the families, but if that cannot happen, adoption agencies serve as an intermediary. These updates typically come in the form of sending photos through text messaging, social media, or the mail. Since my adoption was closed this was not a requirement, but my mom chose to do this on her own accord, never imagining that the agency wasn't passing the letters along to Deborah.

Every year, my parents mailed photos and letter updates about me and my family to the adoption agency and asked them to deliver the updates to Deborah. My parents sent pictures of me blowing out candles at my birthday parties, holding up ribbons after winning a race or a basketball game, grinning with a tooth missing, having my face painted at fun events, or sitting on a Black Santa Claus's lap. They also sent my artwork along with a note: "Angela is in 2nd grade this year. She won the spelling bee and loves the color pink." Or "Angela went to Jr. Prom this year as a sophomore in high school. She is headed to the state championship for track & field." My family's annual Christmas card was sent to Deborah and signed by me and all my siblings. We hoped that the photos might help Deborah to heal if she was feeling any sense of loss or grief over my adoption. We'd hoped the photos would be proof that I existed and that I was being taken care of. We'd hoped that they would allow her to watch me grow up, which might lessen the experience of being stuck in the trauma of my birth. However, unbeknownst to us, the photos sat at the adoption agency undelivered, and we didn't know why.

Some birth parents say that receiving continual updates about their child's growth and upbringing is difficult because it is a reminder that someone else is raising their child. This was the case for Sara, a birth mother who wrote about her experience for her graduate dissertation. In her essay, she described a phone call she received from her daughter's adoptive parents when her daughter was just a few weeks old:

> I remember right after our first goodbye and Margaret arrived home with the Bennetts, they left for Martha's Vineyard for a family vacation. Margaret was only a few weeks old at the time. In a phone call with Martha I remember asking the simple question, "How is Margaret doing?" It broke my heart to hear that she was having a hard time sleeping, and that she was colicky. I wanted to scream into the phone, "Why did you take a newborn baby there? Don't you think such a small infant should be home and in their own bed!" But who was I to tell this woman, a mother of a six year old and the adoptive mother of my child, how to parent? I had to find my place, bite my tongue, and respect their parenting choices

for their new baby . . . not mine, theirs. I told myself instead that my
child was having opportunities to travel already, see amazing places, and
be with two wonderful people. Margaret had a wonderful road ahead of
her. I had college to return to.[3]

Sara tried to move on and focus on other things, but the grief and guilt
followed her. "I used to keep photo albums of Margaret separate of those
that I kept of my friends. I would hide them in a box deep in my closet."[4]

People who have unresolved trauma may regress and rely on behaviors
like rocking or pacing or sucking their thumb as coping mechanisms. As I
got to know Deborah over the next few months, I learned that she quelled
her ambiguous loss with a comfort toy. Soon after my birth, Deborah found
a Black baby doll and raised it in my stead. She took care of the baby doll
by "giving it a bath" (putting the doll in the washing machine), "lettin'
her watch her favorite show" (propping the doll in front of the television),
and putting it in time-out when "she's talkin' back."

Nurturing, caring for, and tending to an inanimate object in complete
privacy was a coping mechanism for the many traumas in Deborah's life.
My degree in psychology led me to this assessment, but I doubted Deborah
knew that this was a common way to cope. It was a survival mechanism
that was as normal to her as the ways I witnessed her dissociating, and her
trouble remembering key points in her life. She shared freely about her
relationship with the doll, who she called "Baby Doll," speaking about
the doll as though it were real and truly relied on her for safety, love, and
companionship.

Shortly after the phone call with Deborah, I flew back out to Chattanooga with my entourage (Bryan, my mom, my dad, and a sibling). I
was giddy at the prospect of going to meet Deborah now that she had
fully consented to meet me. I had a goal for this trip. I wanted Deborah
to have the photos and letters that were supposed to be delivered to her.
On our first day in town, we drove up to Deborah's house to pick her up.
She was waiting on the front step. She looked eager to see us and threw
her arms around my mom right away. Deborah and I shared a gentle side
hug. I wondered how long she'd been ready to go, how much care she'd
taken with her dress and hair. I wondered if this day felt as weighty and
important to her as it did to me.

We pulled up to a homey looking house, with the adoption agency sign out front. Deborah entered first, followed by me, Bryan, then my mom. The director was expecting us, as I'd emailed her letting her know we'd be coming and hoped that they'd deliver Deborah the eighteen years of photos that had been sent for her in the past two decades. The beige walls were covered with large glossy photos of happy families with children. There were crosses on the walls and framed Bible quotes. The agency director invited us into their conference room, where she placed two manila folders on a table.

"Hi Deborah," the director of the agency began with a cloying sweetness that was hard for me to swallow. "For eighteen years, Angela's family was sending you pictures and letters. We didn't have any way of getting this to you, because we didn't have your address, but it has been here for you to pick up all these years."

Deborah's discomfort was obvious, and it was hard to watch. I wondered how she felt being inside a place that had shaped her life so powerfully. She held herself still and silent and kept her sunglasses on, hiding behind their dark lenses. When she finally removed them, she hung her head low, not looking up at anyone except my mom on occasion.

Anger surged inside of me. I knew the onus was on Deborah to update the agency as to her whereabouts because it is rare for adoption agencies to proactively keep tabs on birth parents. Sadly, there is nothing to gain for the agencies to do so. Birth parents do not contribute financially to adoption agencies and, while fees from adoptive parents provide essential revenue for an agency's survival, most have limited staff and financial resources to track down birth families. This is a reality I understand, but it still made my heart ache to think how physically close Deborah was to this building without any idea these photos and letters were waiting for her. My mind wandered to the concept of freedom. I thought about Audre Lorde, the poet who wrote, "I am not free while any woman is unfree, even when her shackles are very different from my own."[5] Knowing that Deborah had been shackled by this secret, of not being able to tell anyone about me when I was born, made me wonder how I could truly have freedom or a "better life" through adoption.

Still, I was grateful that this agency had carefully preserved and stored all the letters and photos we'd sent over the years so that Deborah could receive them now. Not all adoption agencies can boast a good track record in this regard; poor filing systems and water or fire damage have resulted in losses of such precious items. Adoption agencies exist at a complicated intersection of adoptive families, adoptees, and birth families. They are constrained by state and federal privacy laws. Their resources are often limited. It is a lot to manage.

And yet, as I sat with the harsh reality of Deborah's situation just after my adoption—how she was simply trying to survive, panhandling on the streets just outside these walls—it made my chest ache that no one tried harder to keep in touch with her. I wish the responsibility to make sure Deborah was aware of these gifts would've fallen on the salaried and re-sourced agency staff, rather than on the struggling, unhoused birth mom. Why don't adoption agencies have any accountability to the long-term well-being of birth mothers?

Deborah was handed a manila envelope that was stuffed to the brim. She ripped it open, tearing the envelope down the front, allowing eighteen years of photos and letters to pour out. In front of Deborah lay years of updates about me, a child whom she wasn't sure was real.

As she rifled through the photos, I provided narration to accompany them. She held a photo of me sitting on the sidewalk next to my brothers and sisters with a high school marching band in front of us. It was from the annual Bellingham parade. I told her about how I would occasionally turn my hearing aids into earplugs during loud events by adjusting the volume down to zero, blocking out everything and leaving me in a less overwhelmed state after having quieted one of my senses. She laughed loudly, visibly relaxing, and told me she wishes she had the power to silence the world sometimes, too.

The next photo she pulled out was of me and six of my siblings making silly faces in our family van. I told Deborah that my mom had two tricks to quell the sibling bickering that often happened on long car rides. The first was my mom's announcement that we were going to play "the quiet game," which would silence the car instantly even though there was no prize for the winner. We would all shift our eyes, looking around at each other and after a few minutes of complete silence one of us would break out in laughter, ensuring a harmonious rest of the ride home. For the second trick, my mom would pull over to the side of the road and not say a word to us, reaching up to the dashboard and clicking the fake red button with the word "panic" written on it. She had pressed its sticky back onto the dashboard next to the volume dial. Nothing happened when it was pushed except that we would all cease to bicker and break out in laughter at her "panicked" face. My mom would then resume the trek home with all petty disputes magically dissolved.

I was anxious to tell Deborah these stories because she hadn't asked me anything about my life.

"We wanted you to know that Angela was taken care of," my mom said, with tears running down her face. "She lit up our lives and we've always wanted to know more about you and know your story."

My eyes darted from Deborah to my mom and back. I couldn't bear to look at the agency director for very long, even though I knew she wasn't personally responsible for Deborah's life of pain and Deborah's subsequent inability to see me as her grown daughter. I slowed my runaway brain, took a deep breath, and asked, "How are you feeling, Deborah?" imagining how gutted and overrun I would feel if I were her. She didn't answer me. Her eyes were fixated on a photo of me when I was four years old. I was sitting on an oversized stuffed bunny rabbit, holding a picture book. We sat silently, waiting while Deborah took in the moment.

"I'm overwhelmed by everything," Deborah said. "I've never had no one treat me the way Angela and her family have. They don't really got no reason to love me after what I've done. They've said thank you to me more times in the past day than I've heard in my lifetime. It's like they adopted me, too. I got a family now, too."

CHAPTER 13

THE "M" WORD

AN EMAIL NOTIFICATION popped up on my iPhone. I clicked the notification to find an email from Deborah. The subject line read, "My 1st Airplane ride!"

Two years after visiting Chattanooga, I invited Deborah to Seattle. I was eager to show her my childhood bedroom, the high school I attended, and the track where I had won so many races, and I wanted to play a song for her on the piano. I was giving a keynote speech at an adoption fund-raiser event and thought that would be the perfect finale to her trip. For her to see me up on stage, speaking confidently and with authority, would provide proof that I had turned out okay. I held hope that it would wipe away the pain of her decision.

"Angela, I am looking forward to my first airplane ride. Just let me know how to get on the airplane and when. Oh, and what will it feel like up in the air? What should I wear on the plane? Weather-wise, do I need special clothes for that, too? Just let me know what I should do!"

. . . .

I spent the next few weeks preparing Deborah for the flight. Deborah told me that she'd only been outside the state of Tennessee once in her life. I taught her about the metal detectors and that she'd likely need to take her shoes off and empty her pockets. Deborah didn't have a cell phone, so we walked through every step of the process before she left.

"Where will my Baby Doll sit? Did you get a spot for her, too?" she asked one day.

"Nope. She'll have to go in your suitcase. Maybe you could tell her it's a nighttime roller coaster ride?" I suggested, having become somewhat accustomed to the important place Baby Doll held in Deborah's life. It always hurt just a bit though, because I felt a strange jealousy for Baby Doll, which seemed too ridiculous to name, even to myself. I knew that Deborah's ability to take care of an inanimate "baby" was not the same as a real baby, and I knew this did not mean she could have cared for me, but she was so thoughtful and tender when she spoke of the doll. It was a motherly sweetness that I'd desired to have directed at me. Often, in our conversations and in person, Deborah felt distant, withdrawn. She didn't always want to answer my tougher, deeper questions. I felt a sort of emotional wall between us. But then she'd go grab Baby Doll and demonstrate her ability to be present, noticing her "needs." The oddity of this is still confusing to me, yet simultaneously beautifully humane. The human brain is miraculous and creative when finding ways to cope with heartache and pain.

I counted down to the day she'd arrive by my night sweats. I woke on the nights leading up to her trip around two in the morning, drenched in sweat, and perspiring through my sheets. Each time I woke in a panic, bolting upright, trying to catch my breath. Five more nights of the night sweats. Four more night sweats till she's here. Three more nights to go. Two more nights of waking up dripping in sweat. One more night to wake up out of breath, and finally the day arrived.

Deborah walked toward us in the baggage claim area of Sea-Tac airport, wearing the Seattle Mariners T-shirt we had bought for her. She hugged me quickly. She held eye contact with my mom and Bryan while her eyes slid from mine after just a moment. She couldn't wait to tell us about each detail of her flight. She told us about the helpful flight attendant who showed her to her seat, buckled her seat belt, and brought her snacks and drinks.

"You know what was confusing, though?" Deborah asked with a quizzical look on her face. "It never felt like I was flying once we were in the air. I just sat there for a long time and now I'm here. I was so excited to see how fast we'd go, but it didn't feel like I was moving at all. I don't know why I even needed a seatbelt."

Deborah had a unique way with words. For the first few minutes of a conversation, she was reserved and detached, cautiously assessing the situation, deciding if it was safe to be honest or not. But if her depth sounding came back good, something would shift and suddenly, with an unexpected turn of phrase or a delightful anecdote, I'd find myself chuckling quietly. Feeding off my delight, Deborah would go in for more.

Her laugh is fantastic. I remember the first time I heard it. It's low and deep—almost guttural. It bubbles up somewhat unexpectedly and then takes over everything, sometimes even her lungs. If the joke is good enough, it sends her into a small coughing fit from which she quickly recovers to repeat the punchline. It was as though Deborah were a child on her first trip to Disneyland, peeking around each corner with barely suppressed excitement. Except, to me, we were at the drab airport, filled with germs, luggage, stress, and my new mother. My biological mother. My kin.

Seattle showed off for Deborah's arrival. Mount Rainier was visible, Puget Sound sparkled, and the enormous evergreen trees that lined Interstate 5 shone in the sun. Flying from Tennessee to the Pacific Northwest will involve some level of culture shock for anyone. I know Nay-Nay experienced this during her trip. Sentences don't end with "yes ma'am" or "no ma'am," and instead of churches on every corner there are Starbucks.

We drove along scenic Chukanut Drive for the last thirty minutes before arriving in Bellingham. The narrow highway curves along a mountain with picturesque seascapes below where on a clear day you can see all the San Juan islands. We passed an oyster bar that garnered Deborah's attention, given that she'd only ever lived in a landlocked state. Even though Bellingham is a city where although less than 2 percent of the population is Black, you'll see Black Lives Matter signs on nearly half of people's yards. I wasn't sure if she'd be comfortable in a town so different from hers. I also wasn't sure if I was ready to see my biological mother in my environment that I'd adapted and assimilated to so well. Would it feel like a split screen where I was seeing both my birth mom in a foreign environment and a foreign person in my environment?

"Do you know how many white people I knew before your family stood outside my house on the street?" Deborah asked and then paused. I didn't dare guess. "I could count them on one hand," she announced. Deborah told me that she wasn't scared of all of the white people in Bellingham because the five white people she had known in her life were all very kind to her.

When we stopped at coffee shops, hearing her accent, the baristas would ask Deborah where she was from and what brought her to the Pacific Northwest. It was always an awkward moment for me. Deborah would often offer more than seemed politically correct. She'd say things like, "I'm from Tennessee and am here to see this girl. She's mine, but not really. You see, I'm not like Angela's mother. I can't sew." The barista would nod and smile but look confused. Another time someone asked Deborah about her trip, she responded by saying, "Angela's foster parents wanted to keep her, but they couldn't because of all of her medical issues, and they're white people! So if they couldn't do it, what chance would I stand in getting her the help she needed?"

I would glance at her quickly, wanting to rush into the conversation and provide context, but typically ended up letting it go, primarily because I was more focused on how I'd never heard Deborah refer to herself as my mother. She never used the words "she's my daughter" or "I'm her mother." She referred to my adoptive mom as my mother. There was no hesitancy or sense of sadness in Deborah's voice or body language. It was just a matter of fact. I wondered what it would take for Deborah to use the M-word. Did she view that word as a verb? An action? Was it an attempt to trick herself and protect her from remembering that she gave birth to me? I didn't refer to Deborah as my mother either; I called her my birth mom, but that was primarily out of habit.

The term "birth mother" was first created in 1972 by an adoptive mother who was uncomfortable sharing the title of "mom" and found a way to differentiate. Birth parents, however, have advocated to change the term to "first mother" to recognize the primacy of the relationship that these parents have in the lives of their children. Rickie Solinger, author of *Wake Up Little Susie: Single Pregnancy and Race before Roe v. Wade*, writes, "Language is a way for a powerless group to reclaim power and fight exploitation and oppression."[1] When Deborah and I met, I immediately recognized her as a member of this powerless group. Her weathered body revealed the depth of poverty. But perhaps a part of me expected this dynamic to shift as we started to get to know each other. Would Deborah ever feel it right to call herself my mother? My birth mother? My first mother?

• • • • • • • • •

While Deborah was in town, I was preparing for my speech at the gala. I was also telling everyone that Deborah was going to be in attendance and that I wanted them to meet her. I prepped Deborah for the event by letting her know this was a fundraiser for adoption and foster care. I let her know that she would hear stories from others who were in foster care and that I would be speaking about life as a transracial adoptee. I wanted to warn her that some of the information might trigger her into thoughts about that time in her life. I also wanted her to be aware that the three hundred guests would be primarily white, wealthy people wearing fancy outfits. I recognized it might be a challenging experience for her in some ways but also wanted her to see me and feel pride about who I'd become. I wanted to roll out the red carpet for her, both metaphorically and literally.

I was standing in the ballroom peeking through the hundreds of guests, trying to see if my mom and birth mom had ascended the escalator yet. My view was blocked by a stranger who saw my name on the program and wanted to talk to me.

"I'm looking forward to hearing your speech!" the man said. "Adoption is such a blessing! Where do you think you'd be now if you hadn't been adopted?" He paused with a look of quizzical wonder. "Who knows if you would've even gotten a college degree?" The gentleman was right; I certainly wouldn't be where I am now. But he was wrong in his assumption about my education. We simply cannot know what life would've been. It's so tempting to simplify the complex. But when we do that, someone gets hurt. Hiding the complexity of the results of my adoption asks me to pay a high price: the price of filtering my beliefs about Deborah and her abilities to parent. Does he believe that education is more important than biological connection? In that split second, I filtered out his sweeping, painful generalizations and prioritized his good intentions over the negative impact it had on me. I looked at him with kindness and grace, while offering a bit of a different perspective.

"Adoption does provide a different life," I said, erasing the judgment about it being good or bad, better or worse. He gave me a perfunctory pat on the back and walked away. I turned to go find some respite by looking busy at the cocktail bar when I saw Deborah, holding her baby doll, and my mom ascending the escalator. They were immediately greeted by an impromptu receiving line welcoming them into the ballroom. I imagined they felt like celebrities. It filled me with me surprising pride.

I watched Deborah as she shook hands and greeted the line of guests. I watched her mannerisms, her facial expressions, her choice of clothing, her stature, her height. Deborah looked lovely. Before arriving, she and my mom must have gone to Nordstrom's to get a complimentary make-over. I'd never seen her with lipstick or a dewy shine on her forehead. She stayed close to my mom, taking cues from her about how to interact with people in this setting. She was even shorter than I remembered. I couldn't help but reflect, again, on how different Deborah and I were. Speaking to large crowds, meet and greets, and such are my bread and butter. I feel at ease in a big crowd, happy to glitter amid an admiring and enthusiastic audience. This receiving line did not seem to put Deborah at ease. Quite the opposite. Her hand looked firm as the donors gripped it with the excitement that I'd desired. But her eyes seemed to dart away from their faces. I noticed my mom's hand on her back, as though to steady her. *Oh no*, I thought. *This is too much for her.* I didn't realize the reason that she looked zoned out was because she was having an aura: a warning sign of the onset of a seizure.

I was staring at her when I noticed spit foaming at her mouth. Suddenly, her limbs stiffened and jerked; one side of her mouth went limp, drool escaping to her bottom lip. I jumped up from the bar stool as Deborah slumped to the ground, my mom catching her head to keep it from hitting the floor. She began convulsing. Her legs, arms, eyes were erratic. I could see only the whites of her eyeballs for what seemed like forever. As I watched in horror, someone called the EMTs who arrived within minutes.

"She had a tonic-clonic seizure," a doctor reported to the medic. The doctor was an attendee of the event who happened to be standing right next to her when she began to seize. "She was unconscious for two minutes and thirteen seconds. Her pulse is 116."

The medic thanked the doctor and let him know that they'd take over from here. I was sitting on the floor on one side of Deborah at this point with my mom on the other side. We'd rolled Deborah on her side to make sure she didn't choke on her tongue.

"How do you know the patient?" the medic asked, looking in my direction.

"She is my mom!" I surprised myself by using those words.

"Does your mom have a history of seizures?" I recalled Deborah telling me that she had experienced a seizure or two in her past, so I told them that she did. They asked when her last seizure was. I didn't know. They followed up by asking about the frequency of her seizures. I didn't know that either.

"I don't really know her very well," I mumbled quietly.

The EMTs continued to ask questions about her health and her medication use and tried to establish a timeline and a better understanding of what occurred. My body grew hot with embarrassment at how little I knew about this woman who birthed me.

I stared at Deborah as she was put on the stretcher and wheeled into the ambulance, my mind racing with thoughts I couldn't stop. *I shouldn't have brought her here. I pushed her too much. I asked too many questions and put her in this overwhelming, foreign environment.*

We arrived at the hospital and sat in the waiting room for an hour. One of Deborah's eyes would not fully open, and the other eye wandered around, unable to focus on anything. Her body slumped over as though none of her muscles were available to support her body. My mom held her body upright, gently rubbed her back, and placed Deborah's baby doll in her lap. While I trusted the doctors that she was fine to wait, I couldn't just sit there helplessly. I paced and wandered. Going to the drinking fountain and looking out the window. I couldn't bring myself to quietly sit with Deborah as my mom was doing.

I watched the two of them from across the waiting room. One mom I knew very well, the other I hardly knew at all. The mom I knew was a caretaker, confident in chaotic or scary situations, comfortable with medical crises, and entirely unflappable, calm under duress. The other mom was completely unrecognizable to me, a little frightening even. I'd watched similar scenes many times growing up when a brother or sister needed care. Except Deborah wasn't my mom's daughter. She was my mom. Looking at both of them felt like listening to two songs at the same time, overlapping melodies being sung in different keys and rhythms. Each song beautiful on its own, but overwhelming when juxtaposed with one another.

· · · · · · · · ·

"Deborah, who is the president of the United States?" the nurse asked Deborah in the small hospital room.

Deborah mouthed something, but no sound came out.

"What city are you in?" the nurse tried again.

"Tennessee," Deborah mumbled.

"Deborah, you're in Seattle, Washington, right now. You are in the hospital," the nurse spoke clearly, leaning close to Deborah's ear. "Do you remember what happened?"

Deborah shook her head.

The nurse looked at me and my mom, who were sitting just a couple feet away in the cramped room. She explained what the postictal phase looks like after a seizure and how it typically includes a period of confusion and memory loss. She said she'd ask Deborah a series of questions now and then would come back in a half hour to ask those same questions again to measure her recovery and clarity.

"Deborah, can you tell me the names of your kids?" she asked as she took Deborah's wrist to take her pulse.

"Timothy, James, and Nay-Nay," Deborah responded.

She didn't mention me.

Deborah forgot about me and her other adopted daughter.

I realized I was holding my breath when my mom reached out and patted my back. I let the breath out.

Deborah's seizure started somewhere in her temporal lobe, which is the place in the brain responsible for creating memories. The hippocampus receives new information and stores it, however only for a short period of time. If the hippocampus decides it's important information, it'll ship it to a different part of the brain for long-term storage. Perhaps since I had been out of Deborah's life for so long, I never made it past her short-term memory. I reached to hold her hand and she looked at me as though she had no clue who I was. I wondered if she had received the photos and updates about me throughout her life, would I be encoded into her long-term memory?

Deborah stayed in the hospital for four hours. We learned that she had a history of epilepsy but did not take her medication regularly. I wondered if she had brought her medication on this trip. As Deborah returned to her baseline, she became increasingly impatient, threatening to leave the hospital before they discharged her. My mom spoke to her with an aching tenderness, "Deborah, we'll head to our house as soon as they say we can go. David is home getting your bed ready for you right now. I bet you're exhausted."

I got the sense that Deborah doesn't like to waste time on negative emotions if she can help it. Things are bad, uncomfortable, unjust, unfair, unpleasant—that's just the way life is. Neither tears nor sadness will change the outcome. This certainly doesn't mean she has no feeling or that feelings don't overwhelm her. Indeed, I learned that she's battled depression and at certain times has been homebound. But she doesn't tend to spend time worrying or fearing other people's opinions or being scared or sad.

Deborah mustered up strength to respond to my mom, albeit with slurred speech. "I'm all worn out from being nice," she said. "I'm ready to go home." My mom and I exchanged a look, unsure if she was speaking metaphorically.

We left the hospital after the doctors cleared her to go. She was still experiencing delirium, but the nurses advised us that Deborah would likely fall asleep quite soon and stay asleep until her body had recovered somewhat. Indeed, she fell asleep the minute we helped her into the front seat of the car and barely woke up to transition to the bedroom. We guided her up the stairs and my mom tucked her in, just as she did for so many of her kids.

After Deborah was situated in the bedroom, I beelined to the dark-wood spruce, seven-foot-long grand piano. The regal piece of furniture took up a quarter of the living room, and the notes I played echoed off the vaulted ceilings. I laid my back on the piano bench and lowered my head underneath the piano, so it hung down near the foot pedals. This position was comforting when I was young. It was a way that I escaped the chaos of all my siblings running around, bickering, fighting, or trying to get my attention. The world became just me and the piano.

I put my hands up on the keys and played Canon in D. Since I was upside down, I needed to cross my hands so that my left hand played the bassline, and my right the soprano. The musical pattern that repeats over and over until the end of the song sounds soothingly like a game of follow the leader. I repeated the notes, while keeping my eyes closed. When I played the piano, everything else melted away.

PART III
. . . .
RECKONING

CHAPTER 14

US VS. THEM

THE ELIXIR CAFÉ is bustling with activity. I grab one of the few open tables as Bryan picks up our order: a doppio espresso for him, a London fog tea latte for me, and a chocolate-dipped croissant to share. I've got thirty minutes before I'm scheduled to arrive backstage and I'm eager to get Bryan's input on the late-night changes I made to my speech the night before. I wanted to update my speech to incorporate my brief yet budding relationship with Deborah. Through our relationship, I'd learned more about how poverty and trauma had impacted her life and subsequently my view on adoption.

"We both know the adoption industry is stuck in the stone ages," I declare with passion, launching into the discussion without preamble or pretext. "The tech industry is overflowing with innovators—but where are they for adoption?"

I rattle off some of the recent innovations in the child welfare system that are inspiring and hopeful, such as Jessica Pryce's work in Nassau County, New York. She realized that child protective service workers have been taking custody of Black children at shockingly high rates. She surmised that this could be traced back to the implicit biases of case-workers and then decided to remove demographic information about a child, providing only the facts of a case. In 2010, prior to implementing this race-blind removal process, 55.5 percent of children being removed from their home were Black, but after using this process that number decreased to 29 percent.[1]

The Mockingbird Family Constellation is another innovation that I love to tout. Recognizing the high level of foster parent burnout, this model adds a "hub home" to the center of a cluster of foster homes within a community. Experienced foster parents live in the hub home but don't have any full-time kids. Instead, they step in to help anytime a foster parent needs a reprieve, a vacation, or some respite. Between May 2018 and March 2021, the Mockingbird Family Constellation supported 299 youths, allowing them to remain in their current foster home; otherwise, they would have been moved to another home.[2]

"We just aren't seeing the same kinds of meaningful changes in adoption, and we need them!" I exclaim.

"You're right," Bryan agrees. He's got that look on his face I've come to know so well. A look that says, "You're making a false equivalence." Although foster care and adoption are intimately linked, when it comes to innovation, the two realms could not be more different because of one essential fact: children in foster care are in the custody of the state, but once an adoption is finalized, the adoptive parents have sole custody, and no one has jurisdiction over them anymore. Any innovations or changes to adoption—particularly those impacting adopted minors—happen at the sole discretion of the adoptive parents. In foster care, if the state or social workers believe things can be made better, foster parents and biological parents are obligated to make changes. After adoption, there is no directive or incentive for adoptive parents to try something new or adjust their approach. The result of this power differential is that little has changed in adoption in the last two decades. To this day, only ten states allow adoptees to access their adoption records.

By the early 1990s, caseworkers educating prospective parents about open adoptions—in which the birth parents and the adoptive parents agree to at least some communication—became the norm. Part of the impetus for this change was to decrease any semblance of coercion of the pregnant woman. For some birth parents, their decision whether to place their child for adoption hinged on a promise for ongoing connection.[3] In many cases a legal contact agreement would be drafted by an attorney outlining the number of times the parties would connect with each other. The standard contract suggested connecting four times per year. Unfortunately, many of these adoptions were "open" in name only.

. . . .

In one virtual Adoptee Lounge, all six of the teens had open adoptions. It was a unique experience for me to feel jealous about how easily they could talk about their biological family together.

"Hi everyone! Let's start with introductions. Please share your name, your gender pronouns, and how you feel about adoption *today*," I said, after giving my usual spiel about how our conversations are private, except if anyone threatened to hurt themselves or someone else.

"My name is Hudson. He and him pronouns. Adoption is embarrassing at the moment because I had a basketball game yesterday, and my birth mom was cheering for me during the game, but she has this certain kind of voice where she's always the loudest person in the gym. It's seriously embarrassing." Hudson was only a freshman in high school but already playing on the varsity basketball team. I'd often have to remind him to mute himself on the computer because he was usually dribbling his basketball while others were speaking.

"Even though it's embarrassing, it's cool that she gets to come!" Hudson said. I was thinking the same thing, imagining my birth mother sitting next to my parents in the stands of my high school basketball games. I could almost imagine my mom and Deborah chatting so much that they'd occasionally miss me make a big shot. I loved this vision. And it was delightful to know that this is becoming the standard for many younger adoptees.

"Since my birth dad is in prison for life, he won't ever be able to watch me play in real life," Hudson continued. "Last week my mom recorded this awesome alley-oop I made, but I can't even show him that because they won't let me bring that into the visitation room. He told me he played basketball in high school, too."

I mentored Hudson one-on-one, so I knew his birth mom was currently present in his life. He first met her when he was seven years old. At that time, she began a pattern of being very involved in his life and texting Hudson's mom frequently, and then, unexpectedly, they wouldn't hear from her for months at a time. Even though this pattern became the norm, it was always hard for Hudson to adjust. Hudson's mom feared the open adoption relationship was harder for Hudson than not knowing her at all, because he struggled to regulate his anger each time his birth mother disappeared. In speaking with Hudson and his mom, I stressed the importance of using the Lounge for mentorship and comradery with other adoptees but also urged Hudson to find a therapist who is competent in adoption issues. His anger outbursts were as surefire as his birth mother's absences, but as Hudson grows, he'll gain the ability to advocate for his own needs. He'll be able to articulate when and if he'd like to see his birth mother and not simply be at her whim.

"My parents won't let Katurra, my birth mom, come to my piano recital," fourteen-year-old Aubrey said after her introduction. "They say that she isn't a safe person for me to be around, but when I'm eighteen I can talk to her." Aubrey was adopted from foster care when she was four years old, after her birth mother had severely and purposefully burned one of her other children in a fire while Aubrey watched. I had worked with Aubrey's adoptive parents to understand their current safety concerns, given that this tragedy had taken place ten years before. Katurra sent many messages over the years, requesting to see Aubrey, but her parents felt very protective of their daughter. I suggested to Aubrey's parents that they reach out to Katurra—without Aubrey—to get a better sense of her current mental health status and to learn if she was off probation since she'd completed her jail time. Her parents weren't comfortable doing this either.

Adoptive parents will routinely cite safety concerns to justify keeping relationships with the biological families from forming. Although some reasons are legitimate—as with Sara, who may have been trying to move on, or heal, without reminders of her birth-parent status—preventing adopted children from having contact with their birth parents can also be coded language for the adoptive parents' discomfort. Research indicates that adoptions from foster care are less likely than private adoptions to have post-adoption contact agreements.

Many American parents of transnational adoptees balk at the idea of sustaining meaningful relationships with their children's biological families. Their reasoning is rarely for lack of want, but rather for lack of information or misinformation about the children. In 2005, almost forty-six thousand children were adopted across borders; by 2015, international adoptions had dropped 72 percent, due in part to countries choosing to close their international adoption programs due to concerns about child trafficking, child abuse, and rehoming adopted children.[4] Rehoming is just what it sounds like; finding a new home for something. Although you may know the term in relation to rehoming a pet, this also happens with adopted children. Ethiopian lawmakers invoked the case of Hana Williams, a thirteen-year-old Ethiopian adoptee who died of severe neglect in Washington State, to justify their new ban on international adoptions.[5] Also, more than fifty thousand intercountry adoptees who were adopted to the United States prior to the enactment of the Child Citizenship Act of 2000 are currently at risk of deportation.[6]

Given these concerns, and the practical inability to maintain genuine relationships, I wonder if we should continue the practice of international adoptions at all. If they do continue, perhaps countries should protect their children by setting requirements like those of the Marshall Islands, which require adoptive families to travel to the country, meet the child's birth family, have relinquishment and adoption explained to the birth family in their language, and complete the adoption there. I wonder if the decrease in international adoptions might allow foreign governments the opportunity to bolster their own child welfare programs. This has been the case in China, whose domestic adoptions have increased in recent years.

· · · · · · · · ·

I swirl the last few sips of tea in my mug, watching the tea bag twist and twirl in the lukewarm whirlpool as I sit across from Bryan at the café. "The adoptive parents must feel a moral imperative to keep the dignity of their child's biological parents," I finally announce. Then, in response to Bryan's quizzical look: "I'm not just talking about the fears about the birth parents' addictions, criminal behavior, or instability being dangerous for their children. It's deeper than that. I'm talking about the ease with which some adoptive parents might alienate the birth parents. When that happens, it unfortunately becomes a game of 'us versus them.'"

Bryan nods. It's not the first time we've come back to this point. And I'm sure it won't be the last. It was my philosophical cul-de-sac.

· · · · · · · · ·

Waiting backstage, my mind is a blur. Normally, I have every word of my speech written out ahead of time. This creates a sturdy structure in which I can play, allowing me to veer off into a topic if the audience seems keen, but knowing I won't get lost and can always find my way back to exactly what I intended to say, even in the pressure of the moment. But today I feel adrift. The passionate notes I added late last night now seem too pointed—as though I'm calling people out or minimizing the reality that many child removal cases legitimately involve grave danger to the adoptee: physical, emotional, or potentially both. But the event planners invited me here knowing that I don't hold back, if I believe the message can aid in the positive well-being for adoptees. So I dismiss my nagging concerns.

I hear them announce my name and find myself chuckling. *Well, here goes nothing.* The lights are blinding in the ballroom of the Four Seasons Hotel Philadelphia. My first paragraph is a basic introduction I've said a thousand times. The familiar words comfort and settle me. I catch Bryan's eye from across the room and a wave of confidence and calm washes over me.

"For twenty-five years, I'd told myself that I had to find my birth family," I said. "I believed that once I found them, I'd understand everything. I'd get closure," I began. "But, lo and behold, I found that closure was an unachievable goal. My birth mother Deborah's mental and physical health are eroding, thanks to a life of trauma, racism, and strife. She has blocked off the memories that involved me because it's simply too painful for her to recall. Only recently have I come out of my denial and allowed myself to recognize the truth. Although I've found my birth mother after twenty-five years, she may not be able to provide answers to my questions."

I dive in, telling the audience about Deborah's recent trip to Seattle, her seizure, and the strangeness of seeing one of my moms caring for my other mom. I note how Deborah's deteriorating mental and physical health make the kind of closure I sought hard to achieve, how her blocked-off memories are a wall around answers I'd longed for. I pause to click to the next slide when someone in the room shouts, "Thank goodness you were adopted!" Someone else says, "Yes! You're beautiful!" And suddenly the whole room is applauding.

I wait for the applause to die down, slightly irritated but familiar with this kind of response. Since Deborah's seizure, the lifelong refrains about how lucky I am to be adopted had seemed to multiply exponentially.

"Phew! Now that saga is over. You can just know that you are where you are supposed to be."

"I'm sorry that you had to witness Deborah's health emergency, but now, you can get over being angry about being adopted and realize how lucky you are!"

"It's so clear that your parents love you as much as they love their biological daughter."

Even though I'd heard these comments my whole life and quite frequently over the past few months, I didn't expect the opening of my speech to produce such a response. Perhaps I *should've* known (there's the "should" again, that assumption plus failure combo) that people would hear this part of my story and immediately decide that I'd been rescued from a life of doom.

In my speech, I'd inadvertently set up my parents as the "Us" and Deborah as the "Them." Even without alluding to any sense of my parents saving me from something bad, the audience made that leap. The audience was made up of social workers, adoptive parents, adoption attorneys, and therapists.

The saviorism attitude in adoption is borne out of this idea that abandoned babies like me need a savior to do a selfless act and give them a "better life." This problematic idea isn't simply a matter of ignorance. There is some science behind the impulse to save children but to ignore the struggling birth mother. It has to do with being cute. Babies are cute. Their big eyes, chubby cheeks, and complete helplessness are a recipe for a dopamine release. "Cute cues are those that indicate extreme youth, vulnerability, harmlessness, and need," wrote Natalie Angier, a science reporter for the *New York Times*.[7]

Other scientists agree: bright, forward-facing eyes, round faces, floppy limbs, and a wobbly walk attract our attention, spurring feelings of generosity and contentedness. In the nucleus accumbens of our brain, dopamine is released, just like it is when we eat a good meal. When we see newborn infants and their relatively large heads in proportion to their little bodies, low-lying eyes, and chubby cheeks, we are hardwired to make sure they want for nothing. In turn, this inhibits our thinking about complexity but turns up the dial for us to provide love.

Birth parents, on the other hand, don't make us squeal with delight or biologically compel us to ensure their needs are met. Perhaps it's because birth parents are adults (or teens) so we presume they shouldn't have any needs. When I think about Deborah's scraggly gray Afro and mental health struggles and her prickly personality, I recognize, neurologically speaking, she is not going to light up anyone's orbitofrontal cortex.

Prior to meeting Heather, the Mitchells spoke about her as someone who had made bad choices that led to her pregnancy. Friends who talked to me after Deborah's seizure described her negative traits as "contagious" and, because I was kept away from them, my adoption was redemptive. This language closely resembles the socially conservative American model for explaining inequality, which attributes poverty to an inherent laziness or lack of personal responsibility in low-income communities. It puts blame on "them," focusing on individual choice and individual responsibility, without recognizing the structural causes of poverty. This is dehumanizing. This means the Deborahs and Heathers, birth parents who meet their adopted children, are an endangered species. Birth fathers who cannot parent their children due to a criminal charge are in danger of having no legal right to a relationship with their children.

Back at my speech, I square my shoulders as the applause finally dies down, deciding it's time to go off-script. Bryan is looking at me like he knows what's coming. I'm nervous to jump in because so many of the people in the audience are social workers. But this opportunity—to be a voice to those in power—is one I feel I owe Deborah and all the other birth families I've gotten to know through the years.

I look out at the audience and begin. "One day, when I was talking to Deborah, I asked her about the days immediately following my birth. She said to me, 'It seemed like everyone cared a lot about getting my baby to a better place, but for me, I just walked right out of that hospital and back onto the streets. My body was achy and sore, but I needed food, so I was on the street corner panhandling. It's like someone was working for you, and someone was working against me.'" I glance around the room, giving a moment for the audience, who have dedicated their lives to helping people, to consider that perhaps their vision of who to help has been misaligned. After a few seconds, I emphasize the last line: "'It's like someone was working *for* my baby, and someone was working *against* me.'"

I go on to express my difficulty in responding to Deborah at that moment, how I felt saddened for how dehumanizing it must have been for no one to offer support, a warm meal, and a bed. But I also felt responsible. Not for Deborah's treatment specifically, but for Heather's and all the other birth parents for whom I'd played a role in the adoption of their children. I felt responsible for playing into our "us versus them" tendencies that see cute babies as deserving of care and adults as undeserving.

My speech finished to a rousing standing ovation. But, since all clapping sounds the same, I feared it was the same type of jubilant clapping I'd heard earlier after I'd shared about Deborah's mental health struggles. But I was extremely gratified to learn I was wrong. As I crossed the stage and walked back to my table, I was stopped by several people who shared variations on the theme, "I apologize for my presumption that you'd been saved and provided a *better life*. I can see now, what you were actually given as a result of adoption was a *different life*."

Babies didn't evolve to be cute. We humans evolved to think of babies as cute. Perhaps we can rewire our minds to think of Deborah as cute? I don't mean this in a pejorative, infantilizing or condescending way, but in an evolutionary biological way. A way that says "I see your humanity. I value you enough to want to protect you."

How do we do that? Invite them into your sondersphere.

CHAPTER 15

THE SONDERSPHERE

M ANY ADOPTIVE PARENTS confide to me that they feel fearful of their children's biological parents. Even those, like my parents, who are committed to providing their children with as much information and connection to their birth family as possible, can struggle with concerns and worries about the impact of their child's relationship with their birth parents. I was surprised to learn that my mom felt some of these fears when I first began searching for Deborah. In an interview, I heard her say that she feared being replaced if I found Deborah. I knew that she also fretted that a reunion with Deborah might be harder than I was willing to admit, but she talked with me about that fear. She ensured that I was aware of the possibilities of rejection, the pressures to give Deborah money, and the fact that my birth mother may not be the person I'd dreamt about. But I surmise that my mother had a support person in her life to help her work through the specific fear of being replaced because she never shackled me with that weight. Had I known her fear, it is likely that I would have quelled my desire to find Deborah. The last thing I would've wanted to do would be to hurt my mom's feelings.

But her fear was understandable, especially when I framed it within the context of my work. I've known countless adoptive families who were very apprehensive about allowing birth family access to their child. I remember speaking with one adoptive parent, Sarah, who told me that their child had "the perfect birth mother."

"What makes her *perfect?*" I asked, steeling myself for her response.

"She has never referred to herself as 'mom,' and so that helps us know we can trust her," she said. Sarah and her spouse felt that acting as a gatekeeper to the child and establishing clear boundaries were ways to ensure secure, healthy bonds of attachment between them and their child. They'd heard stories of adoptees who didn't have strong attachments to their adoptive parents and wanted to avoid this, so they allowed the birth mom to see her biological child, but only at the place and time of their choosing. They sent her photos, but only hard copies, because they didn't want her to be able to easily share them on social media and make it seem as though she was parenting *their child*. They felt safer in their role as parents, with rigid boundaries that allowed for no mistakes about who was primary.

"She knows her place," Sarah told me with a confident nod.

There are no federal laws in place enforcing the terms of open adoption, and since the child legally belongs to the adoptive parents, they have all the power to decide how often and when they'd like to interact with their child's birth family. Many adoptive parents genuinely desire to know their children's biological family, but there is also widespread fear that being "too open" in the adoption may create confusion for the child. And, worse yet, could make achieving a healthy attachment with the adoptive parents unattainable.

Since every adopted child has experienced a disrupted attachment at one point, it's natural for adoptive parents to be concerned that their child might display ambivalent-insecure attachment and avoidant-insecure attachment or a disorganized attachment. A therapist in Eugene, Oregon, describes these attachment styles in this way:

> Children with an avoidant attachment style may be emotionally distant, preferring to play and interact with objects rather than people. They might be wary of physical contact like hugs and cuddles. A child with an avoidant attachment style often displays early signs of independence, wanting to do things themselves rather than ask for help from their parents or other adults. . . . An ambivalent [attachment] style in childhood is characterized by high levels of anxiety and insecurity. Children . . . may seem clingy and more frequently seek the attention of their parent or caregiver, yet may reject that attention when it is offered. They may

also be particularly wary of strangers. . . . Children with a disorganized attachment style often seem to struggle with managing their emotions. They may display anger and erratic behavior, but are just as likely to seem depressed, withdrawn, and unresponsive.[1]

Since every adoptee has experienced a disrupted attachment, these terms became well-known in the adoption community.

In 1963, psychologist Mary Ainsworth began research at Johns Hopkins University to test a child's attachment style. She developed the "Strange Situation," a method of observing the relationship between a parent and child, to determine the attachment style. It works by putting the child and her mother alone in a room filled with toys. The mother lets the child explore the room on her own. After the child has had time to explore, a stranger enters the room and talks with the mother. Then the stranger shifts attention to the child. As the stranger approaches the child, the mother sneaks away. After several minutes, the mother returns. She comforts her child and then leaves again. The stranger leaves as well. A few minutes later, the stranger returns and interacts with the child. Finally, the mother returns and greets her child. Children who show some distress when their mother leaves and are soothed upon her return are considered to be securely attached. They can explore the room freely and return to their mother without anxiety—or if frightened, they seek comfort from their mother, whom they view as a safe haven.[2]

Social workers began advising adoptive parents extensively on how to create an environment that ensured attachment between adoptive parents and their adopted child, suggesting strategies for nurturing touch and other bonding ideas beginning in the late 1980s. Some adoptees struggle to believe that their adoptive parents aren't going to leave them. One adoptee I mentor told me that when his mom leaves to go grocery shopping, he texts her every fifteen minutes asking where she is, even though she clearly communicates with him where she is going and how long she'll be gone. He told me this with a look of confusion because he recognized his anxious fear that she wouldn't come back was unwarranted. It is tempting for adoptive parents to minimize all additional potential stressors for their children. Facilitating visits and times to hang out with the biological family can feel like an unnecessary, complicating factor for the adoptees; however, research on the benefits of open adoption shows that visits between adopted children and their biological family actually promote a deepening of the attachment between children and their adoptive parents. While this may feel counterintuitive to many adoptive parents, I've seen this truth borne out in the research, in the lives of the adoptees I mentor, and in my own experience.

While searching for Deborah, my relationship with my mom strengthened. Even though we were opening our home to another person who shared the same title of "mom," my ability to talk with my mom about my hopes and fears about Deborah, and my mom's active, engaged response created a sense of trust. She acknowledged my loss and created space for me to express my full self with her. Contrary to my mom's initial fears, our bond was deepened by the search and discovery of my birth mom. Attachment research indicates that the best predictor of adult attachment style is the perceptions that people have about the quality of their relationships with their parents. Adoptees in open arrangements might learn that they were not unloved or abandoned, and this helps minimize or neutralize feelings of rejection, allowing the adoptee to develop a better sense of self, which can lead to better communication and rapport with their adoptive parents.[3]

I hosted a family visit between Sarah's family and their child's "perfect" birth mother, Diana. Sarah and I sat together while her son ate lunch with Diana at a picnic table across the field at a local park. Sarah was fidgety and nervous, continually looking over her shoulder at her son who was laughing and sharing tender moments with his birth mother. Sarah shared her feelings of anxiety with me as we sat together. She had emailed Diana prior to the visit with instructions to refer to herself as "birth mom," and to refer to Sarah as "your mom" during the visit. In addition to this, Sarah included a list of other stipulations that she hoped, but couldn't guarantee, were being followed. The tension at this lack of control poured off Sarah as we sat together.

But later that day, Sarah called to tell me her son had said, "That was really fun seeing my birth mom today, but it's nice to be back with you." Sarah felt like he was communicating to her, *don't worry, you're still my mom.*

I was glad that Sarah had received this affirmation, but disappointed that it had fallen on her son's shoulders to soothe her.

Sometimes when adoptive parents react with rigid boundaries, control, and power over the birth families, they are functioning from their reptilian brain, treating the birth family as a threat, rather than tapping into the reasoning and judgment in their modern brain.

There are many approaches to helping adoptive parents quiet their reptilian brain response and move toward birth families from their frontal cortex. Perhaps in-person meetings are too much at first, but exchanging phone calls or texts is possible. Perhaps my mom felt less threatened by Deborah because of the nature of my closed adoption. Maybe not knowing Deborah for the first twenty-five years of my life made it easier to override her ancient animal programming and tap into her frontal lobe so she could be rational, reasonable, and thoughtful. Although my mom had shown genuine love and care for Deborah from a distance, the fact that she had never met her made a difference. Yet even these kinds of "long-distance" efforts are still out of reach for most adoptive parents.

Three years after adopting Heather's baby, I checked in with the Mitchells to see how they were doing and to ask if they'd framed the photo that I took of Heather holding her baby just hours after she gave birth. This was a follow-up from a conversation we'd had at the hospital three years earlier, when Heather, the Mitchells, and I talked about the importance of maintaining a connection, for the sake of their daughter. At that time, I shared a variety of different options for how the open adoption could look.

"You could share your phone numbers to text each other directly, or friend each other on social media. If that feels too close at this point, I can ask an attorney to draw up a legal agreement that outlines in-person meeting terms." I offered a few other ideas, emphasizing that the type of contact and how often it happens differs for every family, but the benefits are clear: the adoptee, their daughter, will grow up with the security of knowing that she can have her questions about her story answered anytime.

Heather and the Mitchells had decided to exchange phone numbers, which brought me great hope that their daughter's adoption experience would be one of openness. So I was surprised and disappointed to learn that there had been no communication between Heather and the Mitchells since that day at the hospital.

"We haven't texted, called, or seen Heather," Mr. Mitchell admitted, which created a pit in my stomach. To know the pain of a closed adoption in my very bones and then have orchestrated an essentially closed adoption for Heather's baby felt calamitous.

I remembered the relief the Mitchells told me they felt after leaving the courthouse when Heather's parental rights were legally terminated. Once the ink dried, they became the legal parents. And since the child was now officially theirs, they were in charge of determining the level of openness with Heather.

"We have stored all the photos of Heather in a box in the attic. We just want to wait until the right time to tell our daughter who she is," Mrs. Mitchell went on. "We fear that telling her too early might create confusion about who her real mom is." I knew she was referring to herself with the word *real.*

When a child is adopted into a traditional nuclear family, the model the Mitchells assumed they'd have, there is no defined role for a birth parent. They believed the nuclear family model would provide children with the best chance at getting a great education, leading to stable employment, marriage, and then children of their own. Their commitment to this type of family model was so strong that even after Heather had requested an update about her child, the prospect of reaching out to her was still too confusing and scary to implement.

. . . .

My experiences working with adoptive families who struggled with openness were hard. I eventually had to leave that aspect of the adoption industry as I could not reconcile my desire to provide openness in adoption with the reality of the deeply embedded beliefs that it was safer and healthier for the child to be completely cut off. Even though I educated all of the families I worked with about open adoption, most of the "open" adoptions ended up looking quite closed.

Over time, I began shifting my educational strategy away from the term "openness" and all the baggage that came with it. Instead, I sought to introduce adoptive parents to an entirely different idea of what family looks like. I offered an alternative to the nuclear family: something more expansive and far more complicated (and beautiful!) than will fit on your average Christmas card.

I call it the "sondersphere," a word I made up based on a term coined by John Koenig in his *Dictionary of Obscure Sorrows*. He defines the word "sonder" as "the realization that each random passerby is living a life as vivid and complex as your own—populated with their own ambitions, friends, routines, worries and inherited craziness—an epic story that continues invisibly around you like an anthill sprawling deep underground with elaborate passageways to thousands of other lives that you'll never know existed."[4]

The sondersphere is a realm where every person in an adoptee's life has a place—where birth parents and adoptive parents and biological aunties and foster parents and adoptive cousins all exist together. They don't necessarily share a home like some awkward reality TV show but instead share an orbit around the adoptee. The sondersphere is the real-life antidote to the adoptee's Ghost Kingdom; a place where their questions can be answered in real time, where their identity can bounce around and try things on for size, where they always belong because all the parts of their story are visible and accessible to them.

I chose to build on Koenig's brilliant word because of the way it expresses a deep and intimate type of empathy that, I believe, could revolutionize the way adoptive parents see their child's birth family. Instead of giving in to our oldest and basest "us versus them" mentality, sonder calls us into our more advanced neurological expansiveness. It calls us to see the humans around us as complete, complex individuals with inner depths as vast and meaningful as our own. In the sondersphere, adoptees, their adoptive parents, and their biological parents build genuine relationships that embrace all the complexity. A birth parent is not judged by their worst moment; nor is an adoptive parent expected to be a perfect parent. The adoptee isn't expected to be grateful for one or the other. In the sondersphere, we don't allow others to be just an extra in the movie of our lives.

When adoptive parents begin to fully practice sonder and are willing to take the risks to build a rich sondersphere for their adopted child, that is when, I believe, we will see dramatic and lasting change in open adoptions.

. . . .

My dear friends Emily and Bruce had modeled a sondersphere long before I'd created a term for it. They fostered their son Neiko for two years before they formally adopted him, while Breanne, his biological mother, struggled with addictions and inconsistent housing. In preschool, occasionally Neiko would cuss at his peers. In grade school, he'd sometimes have outbursts and would yell, "I hate school and I don't want to be here!"

Emily and Bruce had tried many interventions to help him manage his behaviors in those periods, and then they realized that the outbursts happened when he hadn't seen Breanne, his birth mother, in a few weeks.

"Your son needs to see you," Emily would text Breanne.

They had gotten into a habit of seeing each other regularly either in person or on FaceTime, but every once in a while, she'd disappear. This was one of those times. Emily would continue to text Breanne, letting her know how much her son missed her and making sure Breanne knew that she was always welcome for meals, game nights at the house, or family outings.

Emily is a Korean adoptee who grew up in a closed adoption. After unsuccessfully trying to find her biological mother, she wrote in an article for Holt International, "I often have to sit back and ask myself what is so compelling about finding her. Why is it like a permanent fixture, always in the back of my mind? My best guess is that I feel less valid without a natural connection to my origin."[5] I imagine Emily draws on this feeling when working to understand the root issues of Neiko's anger. She surmised that not seeing his birth mom for long stretches of time felt scary to Neiko. Perhaps it felt like he was being abandoned again, a feeling she could empathize with.

In *Neiko's Story*, a short documentary that features their relationship, I interviewed Breanne, who told me that Bruce and Emily are among her only supports. I notice the ways the power differential remains in place and know the only way to decrease that imbalance is for Breanne to remain in Emily and Bruce's sondersphere.

When Breanne finally responded to Emily's text, not only did Neiko's behavior at school improve but Bruce was able to support Breanne's housing woes. He went to the appeals board of the housing complex where she lived and advocated for her to be approved for an apartment because of her desire to improve her life circumstances. She now has more housing stability than she has had at any point in the last ten years.

Had Emily and Bruce been unaware of the reason for Breanne's frequent disappearances they may have written her off as being uninterested in Neiko. In reality, she was struggling from not seeing him, too. The sondersphere does not pretend that these relationships are easy. Adoption relationships, by definition, are messy.

. . . .

The sondersphere is based on the Dunbar Theory, which posits that there is a limit to how much social complexity we humans can handle. Because of the size of our neocortex (the part of the brain associated with cognition and language), we have the emotional bandwidth for meaningful connection with 150 people. We are hardwired to have a drastic double standard for the people inside our sphere versus the 99.999 percent of the world's population who are on the outside. Anyone outside of our sphere doesn't register as a person—they are more like SIMS, avatars, or movie extras.

Early tribes of humans were glued together mostly by family ties. But since that is no longer needed for the survival and the replication of our specific genes, we can now explore creating family networks that are expansive and inclusive. The Dunbar Theory shows us how those networks are structured. The tightest circle has just five people—loved ones. That's followed by successive layers of 15 good friends, 50 friends, 150 meaningful contacts, 500 acquaintances, and 1,500 people we can recognize. As John Koenig says, "In your life, you are the main character—the protagonist—the star at the center of your own unfolding story. You're surrounded by your supporting cast: friends, and family hanging in your immediate orbit. Scattered a little further out, a network of acquaintances who drift in and out of contact over the years."

This is where the sondersphere comes in, providing support for adoptees, adoptive families, and birth families, by creating a network of people they are connected to, with each connection holding different and essential answers to their identity and belonging. Each adoptee's sondersphere includes birth family, adoptive family, and fictive kin—people who are not related by birth, adoption, or marriage to an adopted child but who have an emotionally significant relationship with them, orbiting the adoptee in concentric circles, some closer and more intimate, some further away. But they are all present, all available to the adoptee as they grow and develop and learn who they are and where they fit in the world.

The adoptive parents stay squarely in the tightest circle, staying committed to activities that promote healthy attachments. Birth family members might be some of the 50 "friends" or the 150 "meaningful contacts." Just as with any family network, each person comes with their own unique contribution and shortcomings. Some folks may not show up on time—or at all. Others may struggle with addictions that prevent them from attending events. Some people may be deemed unsafe for a time.

When adoptees are provided with a full sondersphere, they are able to make sense of themselves and their situation through actual experience, rather than the painful perils of existing in a Ghost Kingdom. While it may be hard to see some members of their sondersphere struggle, the sphere also offers them the chance to deal with this reality with the safe support of their adoptive family. If I had been able to build my sondersphere as I was growing up, I would have seen some of Deborah's struggle firsthand. Her dissociative tendencies may have precluded her from a close, strong, or constant relationship with me, but seeing her inability to be consistent and her medical struggles would have offered me a true glimpse into her life. As I came to see how these struggles prevented her from being able to parent me, I could have processed this with my mom and dad.

In my sondersphere, Deborah would not only have been invited to our grand Christmas gatherings—where the door is always open to my former foster siblings, exchange students who traveled across the world to live with us for extended periods of time, neighbors, and significant others—but perhaps she'd also have picked me up and taken me to piano lessons or sat in the stands during my basketball games from time to time. Deborah would have joined other fictive kin who were already inside my sondersphere. Fictive kin relationships are a great example of the elasticity of family roles. They were a survival tool for African families who were marred by the institution of slavery. They prospered by embracing nonlineal ties and began referring to each other as "brother," "sister," or "auntie," as a sign of familial solidarity. Mentors, coaches, teachers, and other fictive kinship would also be considered part of this expansive family. In this arrangement, it's likely that Deborah would have gained a support network, too. Perhaps someone within my sondersphere would know of a therapist who could treat complex PTSD, and someone else might be willing to help pay for the sessions. If Deborah had been part of my sondersphere, I may not have spent as much time in my Ghost Kingdom. I likely would have spent more time living in the present and integrating the truth about the need for my adoption. It would have negated a need for me to fly across the country at age twenty-five seeking a hopeful reunion that turned into a traumatic rejection, and perhaps Nay-Nay, James, Timothy, and I may have been able to get to know each other at Camp To Belong, a summer camp for siblings who were separated because of foster care or adoption. My sondersphere was beginning to form though, as I watched my dad help Deborah onto the back of his motorcycle before they drove through town for a joyride together. It reminded me of the time when I rode on the back of my dad's motorcycle to my first day of school. To see Deborah experiencing this solidified that she had arrived. She was in my sondersphere.

I am hopeful that the adoptive community's embrace of the sonder-sphere will lead to more families like Emily, Bruce, Neiko, and Breanne's. Or that adoptees can feel in charge of the biological relationships they sometimes need distance from and that they can make decisions about meeting their birth family members intentionally and with evidence. This volition over their own lives can dramatically improve adoptees' experience of finding identity and belonging as they grow up. I have seen it make all the difference for adoptees I mentor. I know it would have made all the difference for me.

I dug my Child Study out from the closet the other day to show it to a friend. As I did so, it dawned on me that the prominence of those three typewritten pages in my life has faded. The study is still carefully placed in a sheet protector and within a binder to ensure it doesn't get damaged. It will always be an important part of my story. But it now lives on the dusty top shelf in a closet. Gone are the days of it staring me in the eye all day from its frame on the wall or spending evenings curled up in bed poring over the pages. As I've come to know Deborah, the good and the bad, my real-life experience has begun to fill the hole in me I'd tried to satisfy with the yellowed pages of my heavily redacted Child Study.

Ultimately, this is what the sondersphere offers adoptees: a life free of the Ghost Kingdom fantasies that shackle them to this day; a life based on real relationships, not typewritten, yellowing pages; a life of belonging.

CHAPTER 16

AN OUT-OF-BOUNDS LOVE

G RATITUDE IS A complicated word for me, as it is for most adoptees. Being grateful, so often coupled with that tricky word "should," has too often been the imposed refrain of adoptees' lives. I've heard so many teenaged adoptees rail against this word and phrase, effectively saying, with a particular angst and vigor that comes only in adolescence, "Don't tell me to be grateful!"

And yet, as I reflect on my journey, I am grateful. In my routine practice of gratitude, I have made a habit of sending cards via snail mail to those for whom I'm thankful. I find the practice grounding and is a helpful barrier against allowing toxicity to remain in my life for longer than necessary. In this practice, I've been surprised to discover some of the things for which I'm genuinely grateful. More often than I'd expected, they are things that caused pain in the moment. I was shocked the first time it dawned on me that I am grateful to have witnessed Deborah's tendency to dissociate while she talks to me. I'm also grateful to learn that she didn't raise any of the children she birthed. I'm grateful to have seen her have a seizure firsthand as a direct result of not taking her medication.

I am grateful for all this because I finally understand why there was a need for me to be adopted. I only wish I hadn't had to wait two and a half decades for this understanding. I wish I'd had the opportunity to learn this when I was a kid.

. . . .

As I click on my camera, I see that five people have already logged in to the Adoptee Lounge. I love meeting with this group because they all have sondersphere-type adoptions. I am encouraged and challenged by how different their experiences are from mine at their age. My computer screen has the standard rules on the screen, asking each of them to turn on their videos and share their gender pronouns and the city or state where they live in the chat box.

"Everything that is shared here, stays here. I will not share anything with your parents, but if you threaten to hurt yourself or someone else, I will share that," I say, ending the scripted portion of the opening spiel.

The introductions always include a non-adoption-related question. Today's question asks them to share the weirdest thing they've ever eaten. Giggling ensues. Tyler answers on behalf of his biological mother: "In jail, my momma showed me what she ate for lunch. My momma and mom couldn't even figure out what she was eating! It looked like a cross between oatmeal and chicken. It was chunky, but kinda blended." Everyone groaned, grossed out by the image. Tyler used the words "mom," "momma," and "mother" to refer to his adoptive moms and his birth mother. It was notable to me that no one in the Lounge needed clarification. Everyone could tell which mom he was talking about because his inflection changed just a bit and it was normal for them to hear biological family be incorporated so easily in conversation.

Tyler went on, clearly delighted by the horrified faces of his fellow adoptees. "It's so gross, but my momma says she eats it even though she doesn't even know what it is." To the other adoptees on the call, Tyler's story is remarkable because of the unidentifiable chicken mash; to me, what's remarkable is his ease in integrating all three of his mothers seamlessly into his sondersphere.

Marley, a nineteen-year-old girl was in the Adoptee Lounge for the first time, after she sent me a message through Instagram:

Do you have any resources or literature to help an adopted kid learn to open their heart and mind up to love? I was adopted at 18 by my band teacher, and I really struggle with all the baggage and trauma I carry and am working on to this day. It's so hard to trust that my parents love me and will never leave me like all the foster families and my biological parents. No therapist ever knows how to help me with this, and I just really wanted to reach out to see if this makes any sense. I've never met any other adopted or foster kids, so that's why I'm reaching out to you.

I mentored Marley one-on-one before inviting her to this Lounge. She was eager to meet other adopted people.

"My name is Marley," she said to the group. "I use she and her pronouns. I don't technically have an open adoption like the rest of you, but it's because seeing my biological parents is really bad for my mental health." Marley shared with the group that last year she had been adopted by her band teacher, and that she's been able to form healthy attachments with her new parents, who support her decision to keep her biological parents out of her life. However, they do remain in her sondersphere.

"My parents understand that my fears relating to being abandoned and replaced come from my biological parents and former foster parents, so they are always doing things to show me and tell me that I'm part of their family," she said.

Marley's parents recently learned they were pregnant with their first biological child. Some of her aunts and uncles congratulated them by saying, "You're going to be great parents!" to which they responded, "We already are parents." Even though people knew the comments referred to them being good parents of their first newborn baby, they knew how this sounded to Marley. Marley is their baby, even though they adopted her when she was a teenager. For her, the feeling of being replaced or not good enough is always palpable. Her parents went so far as to remove people from their sondersphere if they weren't able to remember that Marley was just as much their daughter as if she were their biological child. Marley's parents were not allowing anyone to ignore her life prior to when she joined their family; they were working to integrate it into their everyday lives. Talking about her biological family was not off limits—it was welcomed—so long as Marley was in a safe head space to hear it. Marley was in complete control of who was admitted to her sondersphere. The ability to articulate a need for physical space from both biological parents and adoptive parents is what helps adoptees feel a sense of control in their lives.

"I know some of you wish that you could've been in a relationship with your biological parents sooner. I wish that I could've found my adoptive parents, sooner," Marley said.

I see lots of nodding heads on my screen as the other adoptees seem to reflect on their own version of how their lives would've been different without adoption. Antwone chimes in. "Sally told me she is sad she can't be my full-time mom but says that I would've somehow had to live without my Air Jordans because she wouldn't have been able to afford them," he intones, shaking his head. "That would totally suck because I'm a sneakerhead!" He turns his camera around to show us his impressive collection of shoe boxes. I'm amazed and encouraged at how Tyler, Antwone, and Marley contemplate the complexities of their adoptions. Their sondersphere has allowed them the room to process these nuanced realities as developmentally appropriate at each stage of their life.

Bennett, a boy with a young Justin Bieber-type hairstyle, typed a question in the chat. "How do you refer to your birth parents when you're hanging out with them?"

"I just call them by their first name," Tyler typed into the chat box.

"I don't hang out with them anymore, but Angela knows that I refer to them as my egg and sperm donor," Marley typed.

"My birth dad is kinda like a mentor, I guess. I mean he's not my dad, because I already have one. When people ask who he is I tell them he's just another person who loves me," Bennett said in answer to his own question.

"What about you, Angela?" Bennett asked. I note the surprised look on their faces when I shared that I vacillate between calling her Deborah and "birth mom."

"That's cold, Angela!" Tyler exclaimed, as all the others pile on in agreement.

The kids have integrated their birth family into their lives in a way that is notably different from older adoptees like me who have been mired with the harmful repercussions of closed adoptions. Their reaction was mostly a chance to tease me, of course, but the genuine shock on their faces stayed with me. I realize I've never asked Deborah directly how she'd like me to refer to her. Had I precluded a closer, more loving relationship with her by assuming she'd wanted more distance? Could I show my willingness with something as simple as calling her "mom" if that's what she wanted?

I decided to call her up to ask, thinking I'd ease in with a fairly simple question. A question that was substantive yet wouldn't require a great deal of thought. Whenever I spoke to Deborah, I became part investigator, part stranger, part daughter. These split identities are exactly what the boys in the Lounge don't quite understand, given that they've had ample opportunity to integrate their identities in relation to all their parents.

"Deborah?" I asked and then paused for her coughing fit to die down. "Did you grow up dreaming of becoming a mother someday?"

"Oh no. No," she responded without hesitation, and my heart landed somewhere near my feet. "I never wanted to be a mom."

As I struggled to come up with a response, she delivered the final blow: "I don't like kids."

I've come to expect bluntness from Deborah. It's often jarring, because I'm used to people gently avoiding the truth—or at least softening it—if they think their words may cause pain. But Deborah's responses are always straightforward. I'm not sure that she interprets her words in relation to how they impact others, but they can still hurt. And this did. It hurt, bad.

When I ask anything about her pregnancy with me, she'll say, "I don't remember that." I've learned that she did not tell a single soul about her pregnancy. When I ask if she's had a seizure recently, she'll say, "Yeah, the world did go black the other day. But that's because God didn't want me to remember that day. Just like how my world went black for a long time after you got adopted. I think I just sat in my house by myself for a few years. But God don't want me to remember stuff like that."

In those moments with Deborah, I feel like a grand experiment in nature versus nurture, as though I'm the real-life version of the 1998 movie *The Truman Show*. The premise of the film is an overt critique of the media's invasion into private lives. The main character, Truman, grows up on camera, unaware that his life is a continuous broadcast and his hometown is an elaborate set. As he awakens to this truth, he begins to question his identity, claim his origins, and determine his future. Though allegorical in all kinds of ways, Truman's struggle for agency resonates with me, as there are moments when my life feels similarly staged. The relentless curiosity, evidenced by continual microaggressions, people's voyeuristic impulses into my life and their deep interest in my dual identities can make it feel as though I'm in a "show within a show."

Truman was born on camera, footage in the show depicts only a floating fetus, no laboring mother to humanize his profane beginnings. Similarly, I lived in an idyllic home with pleasant people all around but couldn't ever quite grasp how I got there. Deborah doesn't have any photos of her pregnancy, nor does she have any recollection of that time. It's like I was plopped down into a make-believe world, and, at some point, I'd hit the edge of the world like Truman.

When Deborah said so clearly and simply that she had never wanted me, it was a *Truman Show* moment for me. I felt like I hit the end of the world. The make-believe had run out. The hope that Deborah could be "another person who loves me" had been dashed. Like Truman, I see that I've longed for a love that is out of bounds.

Reviewing my actions over the past ten years of knowing Deborah, I suddenly feel like I've ignored a key piece of the puzzle this whole time. I'd been ascribing motivations and emotions to Deborah that she never actually expressed. I'd projected the desires and wishes of all of the pregnant women I was working with who reluctantly, ashamedly, unfairly place their child for adoption. Somehow, in all those years, I'd never asked Deborah about her own wants and desires.

When she first denied me, even though I gave her space, I'd assumed she simply needed time to tell her family about me and deal with the backlash before choosing to invite me into her life. When she met my parents and told them "You were meant to have her," I decided she must've felt oppressed and unable to speak up against these white, more affluent people standing in front of her. I thought about the pictures and letters that she received at the adoption agency. She didn't smile upon receiving them, but I thought that may have been because she was embarrassed about her teeth or harbored deep resentment toward that adoption agency and the social worker. I decided it was a triggering space for her. It is rare that she asks questions about my upbringing, but I rationalized that it may feel insulting to think about what my adoptive parents provided for me, knowing that she couldn't have done it.

But now she's telling me a different story. A story that sears at my very core. Deborah is telling me very clearly that she simply never wanted to be a mom. Or as each shallow beat of my heart seems to whisper, she never wanted me.

Although I've heard many stories of birth parents who didn't want to *meet* their children, I hadn't really considered that those birth parents never wanted to be a parent at all. But at the same time, I know many adults who have chosen a child-free life. In fact, Bryan and I are those people. In happy defiance of societal norms, we put energy that could have gone toward parenting into our friends' kids, providing occasional respite for the parents of our nieces and nephews, and spoiling Grandma Pearl (our cat). We love this life and see it as our right to choose this for ourselves. Yet I'd never extended that same consideration to Deborah; I'd somehow never imagined that she could have held the same desire.

Even though I never imagined Deborah's pregnancy with me was planned, I'd still assumed that she would've wanted to parent me if the circumstances were different. For some reason, I placed the very societal pressures I so detested for myself on Deborah. *She's a woman of child-bearing age, of course she'd want to become a mom!* Perhaps, on some level, I'd bought into the idea that autonomy and agency are the purview of the middle and upper classes only. I can't help but wonder whether this, too, is the result of a life lived in my Ghost Kingdom where Deborah was never a real person but was painted in great detail by my young imagination. If I had been part of a full sondersphere, could I have come to understand Deborah's nuances and complexities earlier and in less painful ways?

After talking with Deborah, I hang up rather quickly, retreating into myself for a while as this fresh assault on my lifelong wound opens up a new iteration of pain. I am grateful for therapy. For Bryan. For my mom. For music. For Pachelbel's Canon.

In the following days, I ponder endlessly on whether I held any importance to Deborah at any stage of my life—from conception to now. Most evidence seems to point to no. But I keep thinking, what about the doll? Isn't Deborah's sensitive and nurturing presence to her Baby Doll clear proof that she is projecting the parental behavior that she couldn't bestow upon me to an inanimate object?

And then I get an idea. I still have so many questions and Deborah has so many walls. What if there was a way to make it easier for her to talk to me about herself? I wait a couple weeks to call her again. This time, I tell her I'm writing about adoption and need the perspective of a birth mother. "A character in my book, let's call her Dee, is speaking at an event about how it feels twenty-five years after placing her child for adoption. What do you think she'd say?"

Without hesitation, Deborah responds. "Dee probably feels bad because she had to miss so much, but she knows that she needed to miss everything in order to give that baby what they needed. She might also feel proud of herself because she broke the cycle of poverty."

And there it is. I finally figured out how to unlock the key to Deborah's memory: fictionalize and depersonalize it. Let her talk about someone else. Dee, not Deborah. Baby Doll, not Angela.

Now phone conversations between the two of us almost always include Baby Doll and Dee.

"Dee would probably feel like she's lost the right to be in her child's life in the future," Deborah says.

. . . .

I grab my iPhone and open up Spotify. I click on the playlist that I titled "Repeaters." Still first on the list is "Acoustic #3" (from that road trip from Washington State to central Mexico). To this day, I use music to move through the toughest emotions and experiences.

I scroll through the songs and land on "It's OK," a ballad written by Nightbirde. Nightbirde performed this original song on the *America's Got Talent* stage during her public battle with cancer. She told the judges of the show, "You can't wait until life isn't hard anymore before you decide to be happy."

After listening to it on repeat for thirty minutes, I lie on the piano bench with my head underneath, next to the pedals, and play along. Most songs' home base is the last note or the first note in every four-bar loop. As I play, I realize that "It's OK" has the same chord progression as "Acoustic #3" and Canon in D. G-C-D, the home chords. For most of my life, I've been soothing my longing for home with the G-C-D chords. I rock myself to sleep listening to these chords repeatedly. It is soothing. It was home. But now I'm ready to sit facing upright on the piano. I turn right side up and find the sheet music for "See You Again" by Wiz Khalifa. I'm ready to deviate from repeating the soothing familiar parts of one song and embrace the heightened emotions of a less familiar one. I'm ready to embrace the fullness of the song, including the bridge, those uncomfortable, contrasting segues.

I'm ready to embrace the complexities of life.

GRATITUDE

Y OU ARE HOLDING THIS BOOK in your hands thanks to my supportive sondersphere. I want to start by thanking my husband, Bryan, who believed that my story was one worth sharing long before I did. Thank you for the bottomless London Fog lattes that fueled me and for your thoughtful feedback at all stages of seeing this book come to life. Mom and Dad, thank you for nurturing me and my endless curiosity about the world and humanity. I am forever grateful for the way you listen to my ideas and worldview. Thank you to Pamela, Harriet, Marjorie, Jay, Vann, Rickie, and the entire Bell family for accepting me into your lives with open arms. Knowing you has made Sandy and G-Mama's deaths a bit more bearable. Nay-Nay and Timothy, you are the siblings I'd longed for. James, you were too. I simply can't believe you're no longer here. I loved your humor and our FaceTime talks, and I'm forever saddened that your Seattle trip didn't get to come to fruition. Alison and John, thank you for always including me in your family.

I owe much of my growth as an adoptee to the scholarship of adoption researchers and historians: Abbie Goldberg, Joyce Maguire Pavao, Hal Grotevant, Ruth McRoy, Ellen Herman, Rickie Solinger, Elizabeth Raleigh, Ann Fessler, Kathryn Joyce, Gina Samuels, Jane Jeong Trenka, Julia Chinyere Oparah, Michele Merritt, Dorothy Roberts, Gretchen Sisson, Sun Yung Shin, Dr. John Raible, Rich Lee, Susan Harris O'Connor, Amanda Baden, David Brodzinsky, Jenni Tupu, and many other trailblazers. Your willingness to question and your commitment to engage have transformed my understanding of adoption.

The book would not have come to fruition without the series of week-long writing retreats that I spent with Susan Ito, JaeRan Kim, and Jenny

Lee Vaydich. Thank you for the nourishing food and insightful, enlightening conversations about all of the things that matter—world peace, capitalism, equity, white supremacy, climate change, and where to find the best stationery. Thank you, Dr. Rachel Harding, and Sheila Ater Capestany for mentoring me, holding me accountable, and encouraging me to think deeper. Your generosity of time and your grace-filled view of the world have propelled my ability to forgive and integrate some of the hurt that I've experienced. Rachel, thank you for introducing me to Scott Barton, who taught me so much about okra and helped me to understand differences between Black myth, folklore, and truth. I will always remember him correcting me, saying, "We don't call them *runaway slaves*; we call them self-determining sojourners, because that's what they were."

I'm deeply grateful for the friendships of Kathryn Hamm, Amy Walter, April Rauch, Maureen McCauley, Nico Opper, and others who gave *Closure* and *The Adopted Life* web series a platform and continually empowered me to speak out. Lisa Marie Simmons, thank you for your attentive and loving critique of the manuscript and to Marilee Jolin, for trudging through the snow to brainstorm the outline of this book on my office floor and for poring over each chapter as if it were your own. Thank you to my mentees, the Adoptee Lounge regulars—Emily, Bruce, Neiko, Breanne, Nancee, and all of the others who allowed me to share your stories in this book (this thanks extends to those of you who I've anonymized—you know who you are!). Niki Amarantides, Beth Yu Simpson, Dianne Tucker, Maleeka Jihad, Krysta and James Strasbaugh, Zora Bikangaga, and the radical hospitality of the folks at Hedgebrook, thank you for providing constant support through this emotional journey. Of course, there would be no book without my friend Katherine Joseph and that magical moment in the Camber coffee shop when she cracked my consciousness by offering a new structure for the book.

I appreciate the opportunities to sharpen my ideas and collaborate with many adoption organizations, including PACT, an adoption alliance; ARISE in South Africa; the Child Welfare Training and Advancement Program at the University of Washington; the Permanency and Adoption Competency Certificate course at the University of Minnesota; the Treehouse Foundation; and the Adoptive and Foster Family Coalition of

New York, as well as the wonderful transracial adoptive families who have invited me into their sondersphere to ensure their children grow up whole.

Thank you to Kevin Grange and John and Janet Morse for connecting me to my agent, Jane Dystel, who found the perfect publishing home for my book. You knew that Beacon Press's history of publishing forward-looking, boundary-pushing work, particularly from authors addressing injustice and inequality, would be the perfect home for me. It is a dream to be a bookend of Helene Atwan's illustrious career.

Last, although I don't know you, Michaela Coel, I want to thank you for your powerful speech at the 2021 Emmys, when you said, "Write the tale that scares you, that makes you feel uncertain, that is uncomfortable. I dare you. In a world that entices us to browse through the lives of others to help us better determine how we feel about ourselves, and to, in turn, feel the need to be constantly visible, for visibility these days seems to somehow equate to success. Do not be afraid to disappear, from it, from us, for a while, and see what comes to you in the silence."

To all of you, I truly am grateful.

NOTES

INTRODUCTION

1. "US Adoption Statistics: Adoption Network," Adoption Network, https://adoptionnetwork.com/adoption-myths-facts/domestic-us-statistics, accessed May 9, 2022.

CHAPTER 1: YOU SHOULD BE GRATEFUL

1. C. Ugwu and C. Nugent, "Adoption-Related Behaviors Among Women Aged 18–44 in the United States: 2011–2015," NCHS Data Brief, no. 315 (July 2018), National Center for Health Statistics, Hyattsville, MD.

2. Paul Ehrlich, "The Two Apostles of Control," *Life*, April 17, 1970, 33.

3. Barbara Bisantz Raymond, *The Baby Thief: The Untold Story of Georgia Tann, the Baby Seller Who Corrupted Adoption* (New York: Union Square Press, 2008).

4. Rickie Solinger, *Wake Up Little Susie: Single Pregnancy and Race Before Roe v. Wade* (New York: Routledge, 2000).

5. Maureen McCauley, "Born and Adopted in the 1950s: What We're Learning from Project Search & Reunion," Amara, October 18, 2018, https://amarafamily.org/2018/10/born-and-adopted-in-the-1950s-what-were-learning-from-project-search-reunion.

6. Ellen Herman, "African-American Adoptions," Adoption History Project, updated February 24, 2012, https://darkwing.uoregon.edu/~adoption.

7. Nick Weaver, "The History of Transracial Adoption," Adoption Network, October 18, 2018, https://www.adoptionnetwork.org/news-events/archive.html/article/2018/10/18/the-history-of-transracial-adoption, from National Association of Black Social Workers, "Position Statement on Trans-Racial Adoptions," September 1972, https://cdn.ymaws.com/www.nabsw.org/resource/collection/E1582D77-E4CD-4104-996A-D42D08F9CA7D/NABSW_Trans-Racial_Adoption_1972_Position_(b).pdf.

8. From adoption flyer for Angela Tucker, in author's possession.

9. Imperfect Foods, https://www.imperfectfoods.com/, accessed August 16, 2022.

10. James W. Loewen, *Sundown Towns: A Hidden Dimension of American Racism* (New York: New Press, 2005).

11. Robert H. Bremner, ed., *Children and Youth in America: A Documentary History*, vol. 3, parts 1–4 (Cambridge, MA: Harvard University Press, 1974), 777–80.

CHAPTER 2: THE ADOPTEE LOUNGE

1. Jenn Morson, "When Families Un-Adopt a Child," *The Atlantic*, November 16, 2018, https://www.theatlantic.com/family/archive/2018/11/children-who-have-second-adoptions/575902.

2. Margaret A. Keyes et al., "Risk of Suicide Attempt in Adopted and Nonadopted Offspring," *Pediatrics* 132, no. 4 (2013): 639–46, https://doi.org/10.1542/peds.2012-3251.

3. Malcolm X, "Confronting White Oppression," transcript from Feb. 14, 1965, speech, Educational Video Group, accessed May 30, 2022, http://www.speeches-usa.com/Transcripts/malcolm_x-oppression.html.

4. Amanda L. Baden, "'Do You Know Your Real Parents?' and Other Adoption Microaggressions," *Adoption Quarterly* 19, no. 1 (2016): 1–25, https://doi.org/10.1080/10926755.2015.1026012.

5. Barbara Bisantz Raymond, *The Baby Thief: The Untold Story of Georgia Tann, the Baby Seller Who Corrupted Adoption* (New York: Union Square Press, 2008).

6. Valentina P. Wasson, *The Chosen Baby* (New York: J. B. Lippincott, 1939).

CHAPTER 3: HOW MUCH DID I COST?

1. Mariagiovanna Baccara et al., "Gender and Racial Biases: Evidence from Child Adoption," CESifo Working Paper Series No. 2921, January 2010.

2. "State Adoption Photolisting Services Websites," State Adoption Photolisting Services Websites—Child Welfare Information Gateway, accessed May 30, 2022, https://www.childwelfare.gov/organizations/?CWIGFunctionsaction=rols%3Amain.dspList&rolType=Custom&RS_ID=19.

3. Lori Holden, interview with Sara Easterly, "'You're Not My Real Mom!' and Other Real Fears of Adoptive Parents," in *Adoption: The Long View*, podcast, https://www.adopting.com/adoption-podcasts/adoption-the-long-view/youre-not-my-real-mom-and-other-real-fears-of-adoptive-parents-with-sara-easterly, accessed May 30, 2022.

4. John Koenig, *The Dictionary of Obscure Sorrows* (New York: Simon & Schuster, 2021).

CHAPTER 4: MY GHOST KINGDOM

1. P. G. Boss, *Ambiguous Loss: Learning to Live with Unresolved Grief* (Cambridge, MA: Harvard University Press, 2000).

2. B. J. Lifton, *Lost & Found: The Adoption Experience* (Ann Arbor: University of Michigan Press, 2009).

3. R. G. Kunzel, *Fallen Women, Problem Girls: Unmarried Mothers and the Professionalization of Social Work, 1890–1945* (New Haven, CT: Yale University Press, 2010).

4. Huberta Jackson-Lowman, "Denigration of Black Motherhood," in *The Disparate Treatment of Black Youth in the Juvenile Justice System*, ed. Phyllis Gray Ray (Dubuque, IA: Kendall Hunt, 2021).

5. Kasia O'Neill Murray and Sarah Gesiriech, "A Brief Legislative History of the Child Welfare System," Pew Commission on Children in Foster Care, November 2004, https://www.pewtrusts.org/en/research-and-analysis/reports/2004/11/01/a-brief-legislative-history-of-the-child-welfare-system.

CHAPTER 5: THE SEARCH

1. Adam Gorlick, "Is Crime a Virus or a Beast? When Describing Crime, Stanford Study Shows the Word You Pick Can Frame the Debate on How to Fight It," *Stanford News*, February 23, 2011, https://news.stanford.edu/news/2011/february/metaphors-crime-study-022311.html.

2. Tendai Lewis, "Colonised Desire," *FEM*, https://www.femzinelondon.com /colonised-desire, accessed August 15, 2022.

3. Helen Oakwater, *Bubble Wrapped Children: How Social Networking Is Transforming the Face of 21st Century Adoption* (London: MX Publishing, 2012).

4. Kevin Noble Maillard, "A Father's Struggle to Stop His Daughter's Adoption," *The Atlantic*, July 7, 2015, https://www.theatlantic.com/politics/archive/2015/07 /paternity-registry/396044/.

CHAPTER 6: WHITE PRIVILEGE BY OSMOSIS

1. Brené Brown, *The Gifts of Imperfection: Let Go of Who You Think You're Supposed to Be and Embrace Who You Are* (New York: Random House, 2020).

2. Subini Ancy Annamma, Darrell D. Jackson, and Deb Morrison, "Conceptualizing Color-Evasiveness: Using Dis/Ability Critical Race Theory to Expand a Color-Blind Racial Ideology in Education and Society," *Race Ethnicity and Education* 20, no. 2 (2017): 147–62.

3. D. W. Sue et al., "Racial Microaggressions in Everyday Life: Implications for Clinical Practice," *American Psychologist* 62, no. 4 (2007): 271–86, https://doi.org/10 .1037/0003-066X.62.4.271.

4. Kristine Freeark et al., "Gender Differences and Dynamics Shaping the Adoption Life Cycle: Review of the Literature and Recommendations," *American Journal of Orthopsychiatry* 75 (2005): 86–101, https://doi.org/10.1037/0002-9432.75.1.86.

5. Jennifer Ann Ho, *Racial Ambiguity in Asian American Culture* (Ithaca, NY: Rutgers University Press, 2015).

6. Tien Ung, Susan Harris O'Connor, and Raymond Pillidge, "The Development of Racial Identity in Transracially Adopted People: An Ecological Approach," *Adoption & Fostering* 36, no. 3–4 (October 2012): 73–84.

7. Amanda Woolston, "Exploring the Richness of Identity: My Conversation with Susan Harris O'Connor About the Harris Racial Identity Model for Transracially Adopted Persons," *The Declassified Adoptee* (blog), May 9, 2013, http://www.declassified adoptee.com/2013/05/exploring-richness-of-identity-my.html.

8. Cheryl I. Harris, "Whiteness as Property," *Harvard Law Review* 106, no. 8 (June 1993): 1707–91, https://doi.org/10.2307/1341787.

9. *Colin in Black & White*, dir. Ava DuVernay, ARRAY Filmworks, Netflix, 2021.

10. Claude Steele, *Whistling Vivaldi: How Stereotypes Affect Us and What We Can Do* (New York: W. W. Norton, 2011).

CHAPTER 7: SANDY THE FLOWER MAN

1. Fu-jen Chen, "About Paternal Voices in Adoption Narratives," *CLCWeb: Comparative Literature and Culture* 16, no. 1 (2014), https://docs.lib.purdue.edu/clcweb /vol16/iss1/5/; "birth mothers, not birth fathers" from Karen Balcom, "Constructing Families, Creating Mothers: Gender, Family, State and Nation in the History of Child Adoption," *Journal of Women's History* 18, no. 1 (2006): 228; stories "are almost always stories about motherhood" from Barbara Melosh, *Strangers and Kin: The American Way of Adoption* (Cambridge, MA: Harvard University Press, 2002), 245.

2. Kristine Freeark et al., "Gender Differences and Dynamics Shaping the Adoption Life Cycle: Review of the Literature and Recommendations," *American Journal of Orthopsychiatry* 75 (2005): 86–101, https://doi.org/10.1037/0002-9432.75.1.86.

CHAPTER 8: UNCLAIMED

1. Jill Dziko, "What Has Adoption Become," *Medium*, March 18, 2022, https://medium.com/@jilldz/what-has-adoption-become-84fc7c67e8d5.

CHAPTER 9: FILLING THE VOID

1. Dorothy E. Roberts, *Shattered Bonds: The Color of Child Welfare* (New York: Basic Books, 2002).

2. Roxanna Asgarian, "A Mother Grapples with an Adoption That Led to Deaths," *The Appeal*, February 26, 2019, https://theappeal.org/hart-family-fatal-crash-birth-mother-scheurich.

3. Shane Dixon Kavanaugh, "Child in Viral Portland Police Hug Photo Missing, 5 Family Members Dead After California Cliff Crash," *Oregonian/OregonLive*, March 28, 2018, https://www.oregonlive.com/pacific-northwest-news/2018/03/3_children_missing_after_calif.html.

4. Asgarian, "A Mother Grapples with an Adoption That Led to Deaths."

5. Resmaa Menakem, *My Grandmother's Hands* (Las Vegas: Central Recovery Press, 2017).

6. Katha Pollitt, "Abortion in American History," *The Atlantic*, January 22, 2019, https://www.theatlantic.com/magazine/archive/1997/05/abortion-in-american-history/376851.

7. Nancy Newton Verrier, *The Primal Wound: Understanding the Adopted Child* (Baltimore: Gateway Press, 1993).

CHAPTER 10: SURVIVOR'S GUILT

1. Rory Mullen, *Chocolate Hair Vanilla Care: A Parent's Guide to Beginning Natural Hair Styling* (self-pub., 2014).

2. Richey Wyver, "Eating the [M]Other: Exploring Swedish Adoption Consumption Fantasies," *Genealogy* 3, no. 3 (2019).

3. Resmaa Menakem, *My Grandmother's Hands* (Las Vegas: Central Recovery Press, 2017).

4. Henry Louis Gates Jr. and Cornel West, *The Future of the Race* (New York: Knopf, 1996).

5. Mark E. Hill, "Skin Color and the Perception of Attractiveness Among African Americans: Does Gender Make a Difference?" *Social Psychology Quarterly* 65, no. 1 (2002): 77–91, https://doi.org/10.2307/3090169.

6. Jill Viglione et al., "The Impact of Light Skin on Prison Time for Black Female Offenders," *Social Science Journal* 48, no. 1 (2011): 250–58.

7. L. Hannon et al., "The Relationship Between Skin Tone and School Suspension for African Americans," *Race and Social Problems* 5 (2013): 281–95, https://doi.org/10.1007/s12552-013-9104-z.

8. JaeRan Kim, "Survivor's Guilt," *Harlow's Monkey: An Unapologetic Look at Transracial and Transnational Adoption* (blog), December 26, 2007, https://harlows-monkey.com/2007/12/26/survivors-guilt.

CHAPTER 12: I'M STILL LOOKING FOR MY BABY

1. E. E. Madden, S. D. Ryan, D. M. Aguiniga, O. Verbovaya, M. Crawford, and C. Gobin, *Understanding Option Counseling Experiences in Adoption: A Qualitative Analysis*

of Birth Parents and Adoption Professionals (New York: Donaldson Adoption Institute, 2017).

2. Susan M. Henney et al., "The Impact of Openness on Adoption Agency Practices," *Adoption Quarterly* 6, no. 3 (2003): 31–51, https://doi.org/10.1300/J145v0 6n03_03.

3. Sara Elizabeth Villeneuve, "Open Adoption from a Birth Mother's Perspective: A Story to Help Educators at All Levels Understand and Help Others Heal" (master's thesis, University of Vermont, 2016), https://scholarworks.uvm.edu/graddis/449/.

4. Villeneuve, "Open Adoption from a Birth Mother's Perspective."

5. Audre Lorde, *Sister Outsider* (Berkeley: Crossing Press, 1984), 133.

CHAPTER 13: THE "M" WORD

1. Rickie Solinger, *Wake Up Little Susie: Single Pregnancy and Race Before Roe v. Wade* (New York: Routledge, 2000).

CHAPTER 14: US VS. THEM

1. "The Power of Wishful Thinking: The Case of 'Race-Blind Removals' in Child Welfare," Child Welfare Monitor, July 27, 2021, https://childwelfaremonitor.org/2021 /07/27/the-power-of-wishful-thinking-the-case-of-race-blind-removals-in-child -welfare/.

2. "Mockingbird Programme Update 2021," Fostering Network, Department for Education, UK, accessed May 30, 2021, https://thefosteringnetwork.org.uk/sites /default/files/2021-12/Mockingbird%20Programme%20Update%202021.pdf.

3. Susan M. Henney et al., "The Impact of Openness on Adoption Agency Practices," *Adoption Quarterly* 6, no. 3 (2003): 31–51, https://doi.org/10.1300/J145v0 6n03_03.

4. Mark Montgomery and Irene Powell, "International Adoptions Have Dropped 72 Percent Since 2005—Here's Why," The Conversation, updated March 1, 2018, https://theconversation.com/international-adoptions-have-dropped-72-percent-since -2005-heres-why-91809.

5. Jonathan Kaminsky, "U.S. Adoptive Mother Guilty of Homicide in Death of Ethiopian Girl," Reuters, September 9, 2013, https://www.reuters.com/article/us-usa -adoption-homicide/u-s-adoptive-mother-guilty-of-homicide-in-death-of-ethiopian -girl-idUKBRE98900020130910.

6. "FAQ: U.S. Citizenship for Intercountry Adoptees," Adoptee Rights Law Center, updated May 30, 2022, https://adopteerightslaw.com/faq-adoptee-citizenship -act-2021.

7. Natalie Angier, "The Cute Factor," *New York Times*, January 3, 2006.

CHAPTER 15: THE SONDERSPHERE

1. "Attachment Styles Series (Part 1)—Attachment Styles in Children," Eugene Therapy, June 20, 2019, https://eugenetherapy.com/article/attachment-styles-series -part-1-attachment-styles-in-children.

2. Ruan Spies and Robbie Duschinsky, "Inheriting Mary Ainsworth and the Strange Situation: Questions of Legacy, Authority, and Methodology for Contemporary Developmental Attachment Researchers," *SAGE Open* 11, no. 3 (2021), https:// doi.org/10.1177/21582440211047577.

3. H. D. Grotevant et al., "Openness in Adoption: Outcomes for Adolescents Within Their Adoptive Kinship Networks," in *Psychological Issues in Adoption: Research and Practice*, ed. D. M. Brodzinsky and J. Palacios (Westport, CT: Praeger, 2005).

4. John Koenig, *The Dictionary of Obscure Sorrows* (New York: Simon & Schuster, 2021).

5. Emily Thornton, "Never Give Up," Holt International, April 19, 2016, https://www.holtinternational.org/never-give-up.

INDEX